THINGS OLD
An Anthology

THINGS OLD AND NEW
An Anthology

by

Audrey Stanley

Illustrated by

Thelma Martin

ARTHUR H. STOCKWELL LTD
Torrs Park   Ilfracombe   Devon
Established 1898
www.ahstockwell.co.uk

British Library Cataloguing-in-Publication Data.
A catalogue record for this book is available
from the British Library.

Arthur H. Stockwell Ltd bears no responsibility
for the accuracy of information recorded in this book.

ISBN 978-0-7223-3881-0
Printed in Great Britain by
Arthur H. Stockwell Ltd
Torrs Park   Ilfracombe
Devon

I never think of Audrey Stanley without seeing her with pen in hand. She has that enviable gift of using words and poetic forms to convey the hidden meanings of life's varied experiences. In *Things Old and New* she has brought together some of her best poetry and prose to entertain and inspire us.

The religious overtones in many of her writings are never contrived but spring directly from a Christian faith that always involves the experience of both joy and sorrow. There are words here to encourage and inspire on good days and bad. I warmly commend this anthology to all discerning readers.

The Reverend Dr Kenneth G. Greet,
former Secretary and President of the
Methodist Conference

Dedication

To our grandchildren, the 'Magnificent Seven':
Louise, Peter and Rachel (Rugby);
Harriet and Lydia (Redhill);
Sancha and Almaz (Bournemouth).

Acknowledgements

Methodist Recorder
Methodist Publishing House
National Society/Church House Publishing
T&T Clark (Continuum International)
IBRA, *Living Prayers for Today* 1996
Reverend Peter Jarvis
Bournemouth Daily Echo (Photo)
FK Bulletin
Nigel Stanley, *A Short History of the Kölkenbeck Family*
Trustees for Methodist Church Purposes
Olney Parish Church
The New Room, Bristol, Winning Entries and Other Selections
The Gallacher Memorial Library, Glasgow Caledonian University
   for the photograph of Catherine Winkworth

Contents

Introduction

Things Old and New is a selection from my writings over the years, including poetry, prose and words for worship. Some have been published before, some have never been submitted, some have been recently rescued and some are very new: a sort of Christian pot-pourri. My motto has always been 'From the sublime to the ridiculous'. This selection contains a little of each, and much in between which I hope will appeal to the thoughtful reader. Religiously speaking I am a mixture too: a Methodist with Catholic schooling and having some relatives with various beliefs and practices and some with none.

Parts I and II of this anthology represent reflections during my working life. There were many busy years when creative writing could not be on the agenda, when sermons and essays had to come first. And there were lean times when the Muse seemed to have gone out of the window. In a sense, the shortest piece in this collection is the most significant. It was after a visit to Easter People that I resumed the writing of free verse – always the biggest challenge. The Bournemouth location had featured the Seven Churches, and Punshon had been the centre for healing and meditation.

In the earlier years I had joined writers' clubs but could find no soulmates for religious writing. However, I learned the basic maxim: 'write about what you know'. So various scenes, people and events of former days feature on these pages. With my husband, I was privileged to serve the Methodist people in seven circuits: Hungerford, Peterborough, Leicester North, Hoylake, Redhill, Basingstoke and Bournemouth.

In retirement I wasn't expecting to be needed (pre-retirement guidance had pointed away from church involvement) except perhaps in a church kitchen. But it was a case of going where I was appointed to preach, and responding to needs for a secretary. We talk of the time when we shall retire from retirement! I am very grateful to the Christchurch and Lymington Circuit for offering me opportunities which have helped to make this a fruitful time.

The Words for Worship section does not include a sermon as such, in the sense of expounding a text; my reflection on John Newton arose from the realisation a year ago that the bicentenary of a significant hymn-writer's death was apparently going to be overlooked.

I have enjoyed writing drama, always in response to local needs. Some short sketches feature among the worship materials here; but other pieces written for local services or for the Methodist Women's Network are too long to include or less appropriate for today. I cut my teeth for writing drama in the zany church concerts of yesteryear. Other worship materials were created in response to requests.

The Charles Wesley Hymn Writing Challenge was as daunting as its title. At first I felt it was not for me, but gradually ideas, words and phrases emerged – and I must plead guilty to having sent in three of the 300-odd entries which flooded the New Room a year ago. One hymn seemed to come by day, and was recorded on scraps of paper (which I still have); and another kept coming by night, while we were on a Baltic cruise. 'In Celebration of the Wesleys' became a ballad of the Baltic, with several more verses. I submitted only five – but I had irresistible afterthoughts.

It's appropriate at this stage to record my very grateful thanks to Thelma Martin, my illustrator, a former colleague in the Highcliffe Community Choir, for her delightful drawings. Her picture of Old Jeffrey, the ghost in Epworth Rectory, is surely a first. I'd also like to thank other friends in Highcliffe who have contributed to this collection: Pam and Peter Armstrong for obtaining special information from Olney.

We have been privileged that so many special people have crossed our path. When a young Methodist probationer slipped the engagement ring onto his fiancée's finger at the stroke of midnight during a Watchnight Service at Shirley Methodist Church, the happy couple showed it first to the minister, the Reverend F. Pratt Green. In course of time he married us, assisted by the Reverend Donald Lee. Occasionally I wrote to Mr Green, as he then was, and was grateful for his advice and encouragement. The Reverend Donald Lee was an inspiration to many Oxford undergraduates in the John Wesley Society (the largest student society in those days). It was our privilege to know many in their formative years who went on to give distinguished service to the Church, along with others who served as ministers and lay people in local situations. (Some smart suburban churches wouldn't like to be described as 'the coalface'!)

I am particularly indebted to the Reverend Dr. Colin Morris, a valued friend from JWS days, for his advice and encouragement to continue with this project; and to the Reverend Tom Stuckey, now living near us in his retirement, for recent advice.

All of my family have featured in this selection in one way or another and I'd like to thank them for the part they have played – especially our son, Nigel, for his valued professional work on family history, and our daughter, Becky, for her help with the manuscript. Finally I'd like to thank my husband, Peter, for his support and for the use of his resources throughout the years.

For me this has been a wonderful year, when all my interests have come together and have been allowed expression: the eighteenth century; music and poetry, fusing to form a love of hymns; slavery, a concern over many years; the developing world, especially Africa, which we visited exactly ten years ago; and the Wesleys, reminding me of that very special time at Oxford, which sadly for me was cut short. It has also been a year in which we have discovered new close cousins and have learned of distant cousins in far-flung places, and we have seen the faces of those whom we might have known. Truly it has been a year of Things Old and New.

Audrey Stanley, Bournemouth, November 2007

Part I

EARLIER POEMS

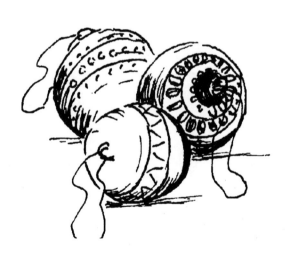

A Poem for January

Today I packed Christmas in a box;
For by mid-January
The berries wizen,
The card-camels seem to leer,
And the grinning Santa
Mocks at the anachronistic glitter;
So I wrapped festivity for another year.

I smiled at the would-be sophistication,
Quickly unrigged,
Of my tortuous floral decoration:
Five japonica twigs,
Three sprigs of holly,
A tall candle,
A whitewashed cone,
A plastic fern at the only possible angle –
Yes, this was all that Christmas meant to some.

How sad the young ones, though,
As they fondly squabble
To fold the tinsel
And hold the blue bauble!
And, "Must we pack Baby Jesus in a box?"
Meanwhile the tiny Christ child chides;
I thought how swiftly we exchange
The festive for the workaday,
His kingdom for the uncluttered look!

"Will the gifts of Christmas
Stay with us?" I asked;
Will the hope and joy outlast
The tree, shining for twelve nights?
Or will our love soon be
Hidden in tissue like the brittle bauble –
Relegated to the attic while we get on with the work?
And will my faith shine,
Thrive, survive –
Endure another unknown year?

Rivers

(To my mother, Dorothy Alice)

Why is it sad to go back
To the reed-fringed Nene,
Where swans glide peacefully
Between black fen fields,
And eternal anglers
Under green canvas shades
    feed deep pike?

Or revisit
The sunlit Kennet,
Watching brown trout frolic
Under rustic bridge,
And martins flutter
For a fleeting minute
Where idyllic cottage brinks
    the larch-lined lanes?

Is it because you are not there,
Nor anywhere,
That familiar things jar?
For you have passed
Beyond communication,
Further than pen or prayer,
Beyond that other River
    to breathe purer air.

The New Look
(A prize-winning poem by a seventeen-year-old)

Fashion – whose whims and versatile caprice
Perplex her suitors and attendants wise –
Enters with timid tread, and flaunts, and fades,
Then reappears anon in different guise.

Fashion makes entry with a subtle step,
Elusively distributing her charms;
And maidens don the garments she decrees,
Obedient as soldiers in a call to arms.

Will she bring colours bold, or softer hues,
A rigid line, or feminine allure?
See, her autumnal debut, unforetold,
Shows flowing fabrics and a new coiffure.

Then enter, fashion, flourish while you stay –
Such earthly vanities will fade away.

Diversion
(Written at Syston)

The mud-splashed board,
Red-lettered, rattling in the wind,
Spells for the busy roadway
Sentence of death.
Protests are raised –
"A ghost town", "bad for trade".

Meanwhile the isolated street
Enjoys an unexpected peace,
Becomes a haven of emergent life.
The young meander,
Crossing at will
And fearing no reproof.
The aged take their time,
Gossip at kerb-edge.
Boys cycle a figure of eight
And cats pace proudly,
Tails held high.

Laconically, contractors
Mend the broken bridge,
Their waiting E-type Jaguars,
Intruders in the haven,
Dispel the air of unreality,
Serve as a warning that soon
The racing tide of traffic
Will return once more,
Reclaiming its own,
Ignoring unsuspecting life.

Normality will be restored,
And welcomed,
For it will be good for trade.

22

Urchin Brides

Today I saw some children playing brides –
Three urchin girls with latchkeys, I suppose,
With tangled hair and muddy socks – who cares?

Pretending in the wind and April rain,
In tattered skirts and trailing curtains, brides,
Where red-brick villas flank the Belgrave Road.

Parading near the all-night launderette
Where girls emerge with multicoloured smalls
And burdened women throng the cut-price shop.

They clattered past, in court shoes twice the size
And fluttered at the kerb-edge, tempting death –
But it was spring and they were playing brides.

POCKET GRACES

A General Grace
(Written for the Bournemouth Methodist Luncheon Club)

As we gather in this place,
Brief but heartfelt is our grace:
Thank you, Lord, for friends and food;
Thank you, Lord, for all things good.

FOOTNOTE: This originally appeared in *Pocket Graces*, National Society/Church House Publishing.

Grace for a Choir
(Written for the Highcliffe Community Choir)

Soprano, alto, tenor, bass,
Gathered in this special place,
Let us say a thankful grace,
Soprano, alto, tenor, bass.

Part II

OUT OF THE ARCHIVES

Catherine Winkworth – The Great Translator

'Now Thank We All Our God' has long been one of the nation's favourite hymns, sung at many weddings, on Mothering Sunday and on numerous other special occasions. Yet how much is known of the talented Victorian lady who translated these words from the German? Reading the *Memorials of Two Sisters: Susanna and Catherine Winkworth*, one realises that Catherine was an outstanding woman of her day.

Catherine was born in London in 1827, the fourth of six children, and she came from an evangelical Anglican family. Soon afterwards the family moved to Manchester, and it was here that Catherine spent her formative years. The children were first educated by their mother, who gave special attention to the delicate but precocious Catherine. Later she was taught by the Reverend William Gaskell, husband of the famous novelist. Another private tutor was astonished at her prowess: "My dear child, do you know that God has given you very remarkable abilities?" His subsequent advice on the responsible use of her talents was a lesson she never forgot.

A long visit to an aunt in Dresden, when she was eighteen, enabled Catherine to perfect her knowledge of German; but it was not until some years later, following the family's move to Alderley Edge, that the work of translating began. Together with her sister Susanna, Catherine became engrossed in translating German devotional writings on behalf of Baron von Bunsen, the Prussian Ambassador. An enthusiast for hymnology, he encouraged Catherine to translate his own collection of German traditional hymns.

Thus began a remarkable career, which saw in turn the publication of the *Lyra Germanica*, *The Chorale Book for England*, and *Christian Singers of Germany*. Interspersed with all the work on hymnody were translations of other writings.

The popularity of Catherine's hymns is undisputed. 'Praise to the Lord, the Almighty' has been sung on the Women's World Day of Prayer. 'Now Thank We All Our God' became almost a second national anthem and emerged as number two in a *Methodist Recorder* survey. Highly valued also are such devotional treasures as 'All My Heart This Night Rejoices', and 'Out of the Depths', which contains the quintessence of Reformation theology.

Catherine was judged by Julian to be the translator 'foremost in rank and popularity', yet she was more than a great translator. In Bristol, where she spent her last sixteen years, she worked tirelessly, visiting the poor and promoting the cause of higher education for women, helping to found Clifton College and University College. She also kept up a prolific correspondence with friends, being highly regarded for her wise counsel.

She died suddenly on July 1st 1878 and is buried at Monnetier, near Geneva. Subsequently two scholarships for women were founded in her name at Bristol University, and today a building is named after her. The tablet erected to honour her in Bristol Cathedral states that her translations 'opened a new source of light, consolation and strength in many thousand homes'. We are indebted to Catherine for her own 'countless gifts'.

The Day Mrs Thatcher Spoke at Our Rally

The recent spate of memories of the former prime minister has reminded me of the time when Margaret Thatcher came to address a rally of Methodist women. It all happened more than twenty years ago, when we were serving in the Liverpool district.

The chairman's wife, Elizabeth Kissack, used to hold joint meetings for the officers of Women's Work and Women's Fellowship, which was unusual in those days. Together we planned a rally for all the women of the district, and it was decided to invite Mrs Thatcher to be our speaker.

As district WF secretary, I was deputed to write to her at the Department of Education, and soon came the reply that she would be glad to come to an evening rally on her way to the Conservative Party conference in Blackpool. Then began the careful planning for the big event.

When the time came, a small group of us waited nervously at the Adelphi Hotel, where we had hired a suite of rooms, wondering what we had undertaken. As soon as Mrs Thatcher arrived, she recognised Elizabeth Kissack and said, "I know you, don't I? I came to your house at Oxford" – and this broke the ice. Margaret Thatcher had indeed been associated with the Methodist chaplaincy in her student days.

We then enjoyed a light supper of omelettes and discussed the forthcoming meeting. Mrs Thatcher approved of our first hymn, 'All People That on Earth Do Dwell' ("I love 'The Old Hundredth'"), but she seemed less familiar with Fosdick's 'God of Grace and God of Glory'.

I felt that we learned a lot about her in that time. I remember being impressed by her discipline and practical common sense – "I never have expensive gloves, in case I lose them" – and also by her anxiety to keep up with the news. The time passed quickly and soon we had to proceed to the Central Hall for the rally.

One question plagued women in those days: "Should we wear hats?" At that time, hats were a matter of judgement rather than the norm. In her wisdom, Mrs Kissack had decreed that hats were not needed for an evening occasion. Mrs Thatcher had brought one with her just in case, but handed it to her male assistant.

We took our places on the platform and the rally began. Mrs Kissack presided, wearing a brown patterned dress. She was flanked by the two deaconesses in their navy suits. Next to one of the deaconesses sat Mrs Thatcher, resplendent in a bright lettuce-green suit. Next to the other deaconess, I was sporting my own political colour, which happened to be green!

And so we had our rally. The message was about education, family life and traditional values, and was just what we had hoped for. The hymns went well and 'God of Grace and God of Glory', sung to the tune 'Regent Square', was a fitting climax for the occasion.

> Grant us wisdom, grant us courage,
> For the living of these days . . .

It was soul-stirring stuff!

After coffee and chat we said thanks and goodbyes. Then our guest was whisked away to the conference – and to 'greater works' – with her lettuce-green hat on the back shelf of the car.

Needless to say, our paths have not crossed again since then, but I was delighted to meet Elizabeth and Rex Kissack again this summer, after twenty years, at the World Federation of Methodist Women seminar in Dublin.

Coping with Being Mugged

At first I tried to resist using the ugly word 'mugged'. For one thing, I did not know its exact meaning. And then, it always seemed to cause embarrassment. The definition in my dictionary is 'to attack or rob violently'– and that is just about what happened.

Last November I was visiting my daughter in Manchester and on the Saturday evening we had been out for an Indian meal. Returning to the car, parked in a dark side road, we were not aware that we had company. One moment we were walking along chatting happily and then, as we parted to get into the car, I was attacked from behind and my bag was wrenched from my shoulder. Shocked and dazed, I lay sprawled across the pavement, and was soon aware that something was terribly wrong with my right arm.

We had caught only a brief glimpse of the gang. My assailant's friends were poised around us, ready to help if necessary. The attack was perfectly timed, and carried out in total silence. The gang fled towards the crowded main street, and my daughter went to get help.

I struggled to my feet with difficulty – already having malfunctioning knees – and tottered after her. Three youths standing nearby realised what had happened. By a remarkable stroke of providence they were able to flag down a passing police car, and to give information about the gang. Soon I was helped into the car and taken to the nearby hospital. It was there that my real ordeal began. With pain intensifying in my right arm, the initial diagnosis came as no surprise – a dislocated shoulder.

The two-hour wait in casualty seemed interminable. A sympathetic detective tried to take a statement – but all I wanted was a doctor. After I had been wheeled away for an X-ray, my lonely wait was the worst time of all. Eventually I was taken to the treatment room and sedated, while my shoulder was put back into place. The cheerful casualty officer seemed familiar, and it emerged that we had both worked at the same hospital in Basingstoke. The bad pain had eased, but I was not to know about the long road ahead.

Robbed of my handbag in a strange city, I would have been totally lost without my daughter. Money, glasses, credit cards – all had gone. Early the next day we rang to cancel the cards. One of the flatmates – a nurse – taught me how to dress: to put the injured limb into a garment first, and to take it out last.

On the Monday morning my daughter purchased another return ticket and put me on the train home. I was sad and concerned to leave her behind. The six-hour journey to the South seemed tedious, as I was unable to read.

It was an emotional moment when the train slid into Bournemouth Station, and, by another remarkable stroke of providence, there was my dear husband waiting at exactly the right spot on the platform. I was whisked home, and was soon surrounded with love and care.

Then the phone calls began, and various people called at the Manse, or sent messages or flowers. One of the first callers was the voluntary worker from the Dorset Victim Support Scheme, who talked through my experiences and offered advice. In due course help was given with an application to the Criminal Injuries Compensation Board.

Our church members were most kind and concerned, helping in whatever way they could. One friend took my preaching appointments, others helped with shopping or housework, or invited us for a meal. We were very touched by the ministry of the elderly and the retired. With Christmas approaching I did lots of cooking – mixing the cake and pudding was good exercise for the bad arm – but waiting was painful and slow. Everyone hoped that I would get better for

Christmas, but recovery was a longer process.

The Physiotherapy Department was a frequent port of call, and I owed much to the sympathetic lady who treated me for fifteen sessions. One particular procedure caused a lot of stress, when four suction pads were fixed to my back. The pulsating rhythm of the machine reminded me of the hymn tune 'Antwerp'. I was preparing a service on work at the time, and found myself singing some appropriate words: "Give me to bear thy easy yoke"– a strategy which helped me through a number of dreaded sessions.

Electrical treatment was always followed by exercises, with instructions to continue them at home. A skipping rope hung over the banisters made a passable pulley system, helping to raise and swing my arms – the right arm could do nothing unsupported. The family gave me an electric heat wrap, which is still in use for daily treatments. In addition, a simple bottle of embrocation has brought relief.

In January, after two months of pain and bad nights, I felt rather less well than when I first came home, and became temporarily depressed. The question was not "Why me?", but "Why now?" Various cherished plans had been abandoned. The Covenant Service seemed particularly apt: 'Let me be laid aside for thee'. I had lost the chance of a little job, and of taking the driving test, which seemed devastating at the time. And would I ever again be able to knock golf balls into the river?

The immediate remedy was to concentrate on what I could do, such as reading and meeting friends, and finding new pastimes. When the pain was particularly bad, I stole downstairs in the early hours and watched TV. I even prepared and gave talks on Jeremiah (by request).

Three months after the injury, as little progress had been made, I was referred to a specialist. He diagnosed a frozen shoulder, gave me a cortisone injection, and renewed instructions for gentle exercise. He cautioned me against doing much typing, which was bad news, as this is my only trade. On the other hand, surprisingly, driving could be resumed at any time. Golf might be possible by next winter, but the full movement of my arm may never return.

Four months later, and I now feel that I have turned the corner. Mobility in my right arm has improved, but it still does not do to forget instructions and lift anything heavy.

Sometimes I think about the gang of four, who gained little from the attack and who caused so much pain and distress. Whether my cash helped to buy drugs or a Christmas present for mum, we shall never know. And I think about the irony of the event – to have been mugged in this way, after having such an enjoyable multicultural visit, seeing my daughter's friends and home, and her place of work. The experience has brought me nearer to people and I have been much helped by their prayers. I am also grateful for the excellent medical care. Although the experience was bad, it could have been worse.

I was particularly cheered and amused by a letter from a Sudanese friend. He wrote: 'I cannot understand how it could happen to you in this way. I thought that sort of thing only happens in Africa. I think the way of the robbers in Khartoum is the best way. Even they have respect for old people like you'!

A Time of Transition

*(A Consideration of Some of the Sources of Stress
in Clerical Marriage)*

Much has been written in recent years about social change and changes in the Church. But little attention has been given to how such changes have affected the wives of ministers and clergy. The French sociologist, Evelyne Sullerot, made the challenging comment that wives of Protestant ministers remain silent in a changing Church.[1] For many such wives, life has become increasingly complex and demanding compared with twenty years ago. In his book, *Methodism*, first published in 1963, Rupert Davies wrote: 'No one needs to be reminded of the pivotal position of ministers' wives in the life of any Church; economic necessity nowadays impels many of them to work as day school teachers and in other jobs, but this can as easily be an enrichment of their husband's ministry as an impoverishment.[2] Thus in the sixties a situation was developing where the wife was in a pivotal position not only in her family and in the local church but quite often in a professional situation as well. Similarly, Dr Kathleen Bliss, surveying the contribution of women to the Church at the request of the World Council of Churches,[3] referred to 'the chief burden-bearer in local work among Church women, the unpaid but often highly-trained mainstay of the parish, who has every kind of duty and no status – the parson's wife'.

Such comments were obviously made with admiration and sympathy. Yet one cannot help wondering whether in the ensuing years the Church has not been too complacent about the multiple burdens placed upon the wives of ordained men. Writing to the *Church Times*,[4] a clergy wife listed eight points of tension and added, 'I can cope with any one or two of these pressures at any one time. But not all.' In Methodism the traditional role of the minister's wife has become modified in recent years, but it has evolved, I suggest, at a slower rate than other changes, and this has caused tensions. I believe that if we are to recognise with honesty, and to understand, the strains and stresses which accompany a number of clerical marriages today, we need to search for the root causes of these problems. The observations which follow are the result of having stood aside and indulged in a mid-term survey, after twenty years of ministry.

In the first place, the past two decades have seen a sharp escalation in the work of ministry, as Christian involvement diversified into different forms. The conveying of the ecumenical movement to the grass roots, the greater attention to communication, the emerging sense of lay involvement – all these added to the aggregate of activity for the minister, and for his wife. And there were the tensions which inevitably accompany change. At the same time as these developments in the Church, material circumstances were becoming harder for ministers' families. As the sixties proceeded, society became more prosperous, with far more cars and domestic mechanisation. The pace of life rapidly increased. Large manses and vicarages were still the norm, with mechanisation coming more slowly to clerical than to lay families.

The greatest change to affect the minister's wife, however, lay in the post-war decline in domestic help – the basis of manse service for many years. Writing of Victorian parsonages, Margaret Watt observed that 'the servants . . . were the foundation of such graces as flowered there'.[5] And as the Methodist ministry became part of the lower middle class, manse families could also afford a resident maid. Thus the wife had time for activities outside the home. This situation continued in many manses until the Second World War. In our own time, paid – though not resident – help was followed by a succession of church 'aunties', but these in turn passed on. I know that in three successive situations I was the first minister's wife to be without regular help. But what was expected of me was not modified in any way.

A historical look at the parson's wife confirms that the traditional role is not nearly so traditional as is commonly supposed. For centuries she remained an obscure background figure. It was probably in later Victorian times that the role of the Methodist minister's wife began to emerge; when Methodism was developing (in the words of Rupert Davies) 'a Church consciousness which grew with every year of the nineteenth century'.[6]

Twenty years ago, one's role was to support one's husband at home, to take a background place at the church, and to assume leadership in the women's groups. The post-war decades had seen a growth in the feminist movement and the burgeoning of many women's meetings – initially the concern of ministers' wives. Dr Bliss wrote that 'the world over one class is being taxed beyond its strength by the demand for local leadership – the ministers' wives who as a class have suffered a decline in their standard of living'.[7] Although the concept of leadership began to be redefined in the sixties, local groups still expected a large degree of involvement from wives of ministers, and many helped to train women for leadership. One lived in purdah at the back of the manse, away from the evil eye of man, emerging only to work with female groups. But any wife who ventured to complain of the sex barrier in those early days was sadly misunderstood!

As the sixties proceeded, many women in the Church felt challenged to widen their horizons. The *Methodist Magazine* carried a series about the pressures on marriage – to do voluntary work, to do a professional job, etc. – ably reflecting the conflicts of the time.[8] Wives of ministers, like other Christian women, responded to these challenges, although for them the traditional role had not yet lessened in any way. I know of one inner-city church where each successive minister's wife was out morning, noon and night engaged in good works. As the focus of Christian involvement turned outwards towards the community, so the wife added Church-sponsored community projects – running a playgroup, visiting immigrants, etc. – to her already full programme. One wife suffered broken health, and the next a broken marriage.

If the role evolved slowly, other social changes were far more rapid. One significant trend which overtook society in the earlier years of our ministry was the change in attitudes to age and youth. Twenty years ago people venerated wisdom and experience, and especially was this true in Christian circles. Then during the sixties, with the growing power of advertising and the increased purchasing power of the young, the emphasis in society changed. In company with businesses, charities, the media, and many other aspects of life, the Church also joined the quest for a youthful image.

In many ways which are not generally acknowledged, this had far-reaching effects upon ministers' families. Younger couples were at a premium, and proud suburban churches sought to engage men at the magical age of thirty-eight. Such appointments, while suitable for the husband, were often much less appropriate for the wife, who was perhaps still raising a family. At the same time as wanting a younger minister, many churches appeared to need a middle-aged wife, an ever present mother figure. Domestically her circumstances had deteriorated, but on all sides people's ideas about her role had not kept pace with other changes.

Today the quest for a youthful image is less passionately pursued, but many of its effects are still present in both voluntary and professional work. Although busy churches are not usually short of lay leadership now, they often make considerable demands on the wife for a social and supportive role. While such appointments are theoretically open to bachelors, widowers or women ministers, people like to see the nuclear family in their church and manse. And it remains an anomaly that the largest and most active churches often involve a wife at the busiest time of her life. Another residual problem for women is that those wishing to undertake vocational training have had to do so while still of an acceptable age for their eventual goal, despite being involved with children and church. Fortunately we are now at a stage when this can more easily be achieved, in the sense that families and homes are smaller.

The issue which has been at the heart of debates about the role of ministers' wives has, in fact, been the question of their identity: are they 'ministerial', or of the laity, or are they strange mutations in between? Probably twenty years ago most wives would have identified with the ministry. Certainly they were widely regarded as almost belonging to a special order within the Church. One even encountered the suggestion in one's early days that wives of ministers should wear a uniform; they were seen as church workers, alongside their husbands. Unfortunately there seemed to be a universal assumption that the wives had been affected by their husband's ordination, and endowed with magical properties of energy, efficiency and religiosity. Gradually in the post-Robinson Church the emphasis changed, and probably most wives of ministers today see themselves as of the laity – ordinary church members.

The inherent confusion in their identity caused many problems. On the one hand, many women were overburdened; but at the same time – if one may commit the statutory feminine illogicality – many knew intense frustration. Seeing themselves increasingly as of the laity, a number wanted to make an ordinary lay person's contribution to the Church – that is, to the whole Church, and not just the women's organisations. No doors were opened and no encouragement received, because implicit in the traditional role there has always been a curious double bind, defining what one should and should not do. Even when these issues cried aloud for clarification, such clarification was never officially given. For many, fulfilment could only be found eventually in secular work. I personally never saw these difficulties as a matter of sex prejudice, but simply as 'nonthink', the sex barrier being like glass with one-way vision.

The attitudes of wives today to the traditional role vary according to their age group. On the one hand, most older women are content to work within the Church structures and would contemplate nothing else: for many even voluntary work, such as meals on wheels, is only performed under the umbrella of stewardship. On the other hand, to many younger women the full traditional role is anathema, and they will not be spiritually frogmarched to the church, as we were. It must be said, however, that role expectations occurred on all sides – from the hierarchy, the laity and the community in general. Clearly it was not only women who did the expecting. Further, most of us enjoyed all that we did. It was simply a case of having done too much too soon. A preface to *Crockford's Clerical Directory* (1973–4) spoke of 'the passing of the older type of clergy wife, who was often an unpaid curate, and the arrival of young career wives capable of earning their living outside the parish'. This is, of course, an oversimplification of the matter. In between these two groups lies a large number of women in the middle block who were reared in traditional ways and have since been caught up in the cross-currents between these two lifestyles.

We have now come to a time when economic factors are paramount and many wives have to undertake paid work in order to support their families. Any inherited money which enabled them to engage in Church work has dwindled considerably, as have gifts from relatives and Christian friends. Early in 1975 an unmarried priest wrote to the *Church Times* about 'the intolerable plight of married clergy with children. The Church of England instituted the principle of married clergy in the 16th century, but it has never come to grips with the problem of providing adequately for them.'[9] One is reminded of the situation in early Methodism when, mindful of finances, 'circuits looked on married preachers with an evil eye'.[10] Until the recent crisis of unemployment, the situation of wives with professional qualifications was relatively straightforward. They were insulated from the worst of the problems. For non-professional wives, the situation is rather more complex. Any work undertaken is liable to be less well paid, and probably less satisfying. Decisions about training and grants are complicated by the itinerant system. At the moment some of us are experiencing a conflict between the long-held wish to undertake further vocational training and the urgent need to supplement the family income.

I have been considering various external changes which have affected the family. The past twenty years have also seen significant changes within the family. The family itself has almost come to be 'an object of devotion'[11] – an attitude seemingly in conflict with the Christian teaching about putting discipleship before kindred. Twenty years ago it was considered right and proper that the whole family should be much affected by the parents' Christian service. Again, this attitude seemed to reach its extreme in late Victorian times. It is perhaps epitomised in the 'Articles of Marriage for Salvationists',[12] where partners promise to 'promote the constant and entire self-sacrifice of the other', and where children are dedicated to 'hardship, suffering, want or sacrifice'. Looking back, elements of these attitudes were around at the start of our ministry, although one never heard them formulated. Throughout the years many manse children have been despatched to boarding school, enabling their parents to continue Christian work; while many others left at home have suffered parental neglect.

Even if all survived this treatment and grew up to be Christians – and can one honestly make this claim? – one aspect seldom considered is its effect upon the mothers. Recently I met a sad minister's widow who still seemed consumed with guilt and remorse at having neglected her children fifty years ago. But the most poignant stories of all come from the mission field – such as that of 'Mrs Mish', who recounted her pain on sending the children home for schooling one by one.[13] The past twenty years have seen a change in the climate of opinion, with more emphasis on family life, and as a result conflicts of loyalty often arise. While manse children today enjoy many material and cultural advantages from their mothers' work, there could be a danger of neglect due to the claims of the classroom, the hospital or the social services department. Even Salvation Army members have had recent problems reconciling their work with family life. A concluding article on marriage in *The Officer* adopted the traditional stance, with the theme 'A wife is a person who helps'.

Perhaps the biggest challenge of all to clerical marriage lies in the fact that marriage itself is in a state of transition, moving from male dominance to flexibility and partnership. Students of the family observe that, with the increasing duration of marriage[14] and the reduction of the child-rearing phase, the future emphasis will be more on relationships and quality of life – on what Dr Jack Dominian, the Roman Catholic psychiatrist, calls the 'psychological, social and instinctual level of fulfilment'.[15] Thus people are coming to expect more from marriage than previously. What will be the pattern as society moves towards the predicted state of 'the symmetrical family',[16] with husband and wife doing equal amounts of work outside the home and an equal amount within – i.e. for – the home? Can such trends ever really apply in certain professions, such as the Church? While Dr Dominian anticipates a great future for Christian marriage, Young and Willmott, authors of *The Symmetrical Family*, predict that 'strains will be inescapable'.

In the ordination service, ordinands are reminded that 'This ministry will make great demands on your household.' It is a fact that any wife of a minister is inevitably affected by his work. Dr Dominian remarks that in the home women have made great strides towards equality; but this seems rather less true of clerical families, where the home is geared to the husband's work. The words of Dr Bliss, that 'the patriarchal concept of the relationship of men and women is even stronger in parsonages than it is among the people generally', are still widely applicable today.[17] Can we really envisage a time when a minister will do exactly half the housework and childcare; and, when his wife's profession dictates, that he should move – or remain? Would such a trend not be contrary to the total commitment spelt out in the ordination service? Further, looking ahead to a hypothetical part-time ministry supplemented by secular work, one foresees less, rather than more, chances of symmetry in marriage. Then do we not have to conclude that wives of ordained men must accept a lesser degree of 'lib' than other women? – or that 'lib' comes to them at a far greater cost? In other words, how 'Christian' is clerical marriage?

The complex situation of many wives today is one of the dark areas of Church life, about which people prefer not to think. It raises many deep questions about ministry and commitment, about suffering and sacrifice, about freedom and fulfilment, about the nature of Christianity itself. Surely God has yet more light and truth to break forth on all this?

Notes

1 Evelyne Sullerot, *Women, Society and Change*, World University Library, Weidenfeld and Nicholson, 1971, p.237.
2 Rupert Davies, *Methodism*, Epworth Press, 1976, p.175.
3 Kathleen Bliss, *The Service and Status of Women in the Churches*, SCM Press, 1952, p.77.
4 *Church Times*, January 24th 1975.
5 Margaret Watt, *The History of the Parson's Wife*, Faber and Faber, 1943, p.93.
6 Rupert Davies, op. cit., p.130.
7 Kathleen Bliss, op. cit., p.50.
8 *Methodist Magazine*, June 1964.
9 *Church Times*, January 3rd 1975.
10 *Minutes of the Methodist Conferences*, Vol. I (1744–98), p.86.
11 Michael Young and Peter Willmott, *The Symmetrical Family*, first published by Routledge and Kegan Paul, 1973; published in Penguin Books, 1975, p.267.
12 Robert Sandall, *The History of the Salvation Army*, Vol. II (1878–86), Thomas Nelson and Sons Ltd, Appendix D, pp.314–15.
13 *Mrs Mish – The Confessions of a Missionary's Wife*, Wyvern Books, Epworth Press, 1963, pp.20–21.
14 Jack Dominian, *Cycles of Affirmation*, Darton, Longman and Todd, 1975, p.58.
15 Ibid., p.60.
16 Young and Willmott, op. cit., pp.275–8.
17 Kathleen Bliss, op. cit., p.187.

Part III

LATER POEMS

Easter People

I slipped into Easter People,
Tasted, touched and mingled,
Lingered and learned.
I had spoken, preached about Easter People –
Yet hardly dared to come.
There were a few familiar faces
Amid myriad strangers.
I slumbered in the cosy theatrical dark;
Was angered by cruel humour;
Queued for wholeness and peace.
Easter People, Easter People:
Concerned and searching;
Connected, wired; wacky.
Easter People, Easter People:
Surging and drifting;
Lost and found;
Singing, celebrating
By the crystal sea.
Dear, dear Easter People –
Come again.

FOOTNOTE: Easter People – a large Christian gathering beginning on Easter
Monday in a major holiday town.

E-Mail to Elizabeth

Dear Daughter on the Internet –
I don't know what to say.
You used to be so close to us;
You're now so far away.

Amazing, though, these microchips –
They send the message through,
And what I'm writing now you'll get
Within an hour or two.

The e-mail spans ten thousand miles –
Just sit back and relax.
It's faster than the normal post
And better far than fax.

So now I start to tap the keys
And think of this and that.
What gossip would I bring to you
If we could have a chat?

Of golfing exploits I could tell
In winds that made me shiver,
And drives that didn't go so well,
And balls lost in the river.

And how the car refused to start,
Which caused a big to-do;
And how the bedroom carpet's come –
A ghastly navy blue.

And how the local news is full
Of politics and sleaze;
And how the garden's hard and dry,
And how the cat had – – – – –.

Apart from matters such as these
All things are going well.
The daily round, the common task –
Retirement's never dull.

Our love to all the family;
We hope they're having fun
And settling in their new abode
Beneath the burning sun.

Dear Daughter on the Internet –
It's not so very far,
If we can keep in touch this way,
From Bournemouth to Accra.

Millennium

What were you feeling
   on New Year's Eve?
Were you rejoicing
   or did you grieve?

Were you with neighbours,
   or were you at prayer;
With nearest and dearest,
   or alone in your chair?

What did you feel
   on reviewing the past,
And can you be sure
   that the goodwill can last?

Were you content
   with the way things were done,
Or are you now thankful
   it's over and gone?

What thoughts did it conjure,
   what feelings evoke,
As the second millennium
   went up in smoke?

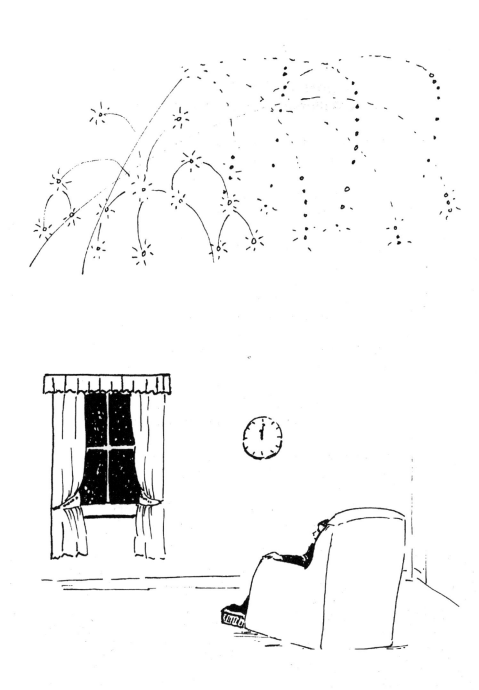

Report on the FK Conference at Willersley Castle, Derbyshire

Pilgrims at Willersley, learned and lay,
Examined Old Testament studies today.

Though Abraham's Heights were not far away,
Of his actual existence one really can't say.

Think not of four 'documents' – E, D, P, J –
But living traditions: a good array.

Some serious scholarship points us the way
And the narrative method is kosher, OK?

Theology: what are they doing today?
Reviving and writing it, that's what they say.

Exciting, alert and alive for today –
Except in the churches – a cause for dismay.

So these were the themes of my first-time FK,
And the narrative method is kosher, OK?

"God has given us a book full of stories – hooray!"
Sang pilgrims at Willersley, learned and lay.

Powerscourt Waterfall, County Wicklow

Leaving the vale of the Druids,
We sought the trail of John Wesley.
"You take the road to Dublin.
You go under the bridge that goes over,
And soon you turn left down the lanes.
At the triangle you can go either left or right . . . "

Eventually we reached the waterfall –
The highest in all Ireland.
"One pound fifty for senior citizens.
Retain your ticket for inspection."
Today there are cars and tourists,
And picnic areas, quiet and discreet.

But was this the way you came, Mr Wesley?
Did you take your horse to the waterfall
To slake his thirst in the River Dargle?
Did you survey the vast amphitheatre?
Imagine it as a preaching-place?

You wrote of the distant vistas,
The beauty – the beauty
Unmatched this side of heaven.
We never found this view.
But did you, too, see the waterfall,
Sullen silver, golden glinting,
Tumbling, cascading, rushing to eternity?
"The Waterfall closes at 7.00 p.m."

JOHN WESLEY'S JOURNAL, VOL. V, P.138: *Monday, 29th July 1765* – I was desired by some friends to take a ride to the Dargle, ten or twelve miles from Dublin; one of the greatest natural curiosities, they said, which the kingdom afforded. It far exceeded my expectations. You have a high and steep mountain, covered with stately wood, up the side of which a path is cut, and seats placed at small distances. A deep vale, through which a clear river runs, lies between this and another high mountain, whose sides are clothed with tall trees, row above row, from the river to the very top. Near the summit of the first mountain, you have an opening on the one hand which commands the fruitful counties of Kildare, Dublin, and Louth, as far, in a clear, sunshiny day, as the huge mountains of Newry; on the other hand is a fine landscape of meadows and fields, that terminates in a sea-prospect. Adding this to the rest, it exceeds anything which I have seen in Great Britain. And yet the eye is not satisfied with seeing! It never can till we see God.

Fringe Benefits
(Written at Bemerton)

Twelve years of loneliness,
Twelve years of pain.

Twelve years of consulting –
And paying – in vain.

Twelve years of praying
For help and for peace.

Twelve years of longing
This trouble would cease.

Twelve years of solitude,
Hard to endure.

Twelve years of wandering,
Seeking a cure.

Twelve years of rejection
Till touching by stealth
The fringe of his garment:
Acceptance – and health.

Istanbul
(November 2003)

On the front of the paper: the chaos –
Ruins, remains, debris, burnt-out cars,
Smoke, fire, an office chair,
A man fleeing with a mobile phone.

Inside the paper: the victims –
The hero diplomat, honoured, lost;
The businessman, blind in the hospital bed;
Limp women dug from the rubble.

Turn the page for the state visit,
The pomp and ceremony,
The special relationship.
Turn the page – turn the page.

On the back of the paper: the crossword –
Trivial pursuit for when reality is too cruel,
Or one is too old to protest on the streets.
What else can one do, but the crossword?

Escape for a while, wrestle with puzzles,
Tease out meaning, restore order.
Ponder a clue – eight down, a six-letter word:
'Wave a couple of pages in anger'. *

*Answer on page 126

Election
(May 5th 2005)

Rough men
In workaday clothes
Brought rough wood,
Hammer and nails,
A notice proclaiming
A name.

Rough men hammering,
Hammering like the men
Of the Crucifixion:
Splintering the peace
Of our Easter garden;
They nailed our colours
To the mast.

The neighbours
Went about their business,
Pretended not to notice.

On the day of reckoning
Smooth men chatted
Anxiously in groups,
Wore smiles and suits,
Fending jeers and cheers
Of the opposition.
Verification, the count,
The declaration:
The future was not
To be orange.

On the third day
Rough men returned,
Dismantled, disappeared
To face reality,
To fight again.

The neighbours said,
"At least we tried."

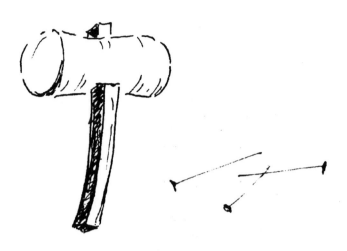

Part IV

REFLECTIONS IN RETIREMENT

Minsk Garden of Hope
(After Chernobyl, June 6th 1996)

'From the Tree of Life to the Garden of Hope' was the title of an international seminar held in Minsk by the Ecumenical Forum of European Christian Women. Timed to mark the 10th anniversary of the Chernobyl disaster, the seminar took place in the impressive new conference centre in Minsk, where the main concourse was decorated by banners on the themes of ecology and peace.

A varied and exciting programme awaited the fifty women who had travelled from sixteen different European countries, many from the East. They were the guests of the Children of Chernobyl Foundation and were joined by twenty Belorussian women – members of the Ecumenical Forum.

After welcoming the visitors, Dr Irina Gruschevaya of the Children of Chernobyl Foundation said that ten years after Chernobyl the worst consequences were beginning to emerge. She stressed the importance of women working together to build bridges across Europe and to help the weak and needy. Marguerite Wieser (Switzerland), chairman of the Bio-ethics and Ecology Commission of the forum, spoke of the 'black death' overhanging people's lives in Belarus and the need to be careful with energy. The theme of 'Women and Energy' was then explored during the six-day seminar, through lectures, workshops and visits.

We learned about the sad history and present situation of Belarus. At the crossroads of East and West, it has suffered many invasions. Of the old city of Minsk, only one fifth remains;

the rest was destroyed in the Second World War. Belarus has also suffered greatly following the Chernobyl disaster, experiencing seventy per cent of the total radioactive fallout. There has been a dramatic recent increase in illnesses attributed to the Chernobyl accident, particularly thyroid cancer in children. One fifth of the land is still suffering from radiation and there is a danger that underground watercourses could become affected.

Along with others from Western Europe, the three of us from the UK had travelled with cases filled with the gifts we had collected from our churches: medicines, vitamin pills, food and seeds. It was very moving to be among those taking medicaments to the hospice. We were allowed a quick peep at some very sick young children, and the doctor in charge talked to us at length about the hospice and its work. Everything possible is done for the welfare of the children, but treatment is expensive. Belarus has only one plant producing drugs and no longer receives them from other countries. In addition to children's pictures in the day room there were religious icons, which would not have been allowed under communist rule.

Following the nuclear accident, a large number of people were moved from the contaminated areas and rehoused in high-rise apartments in Minsk, thus becoming refugees in their own country. A warm welcome awaited us when we visited the resettlers' centre on one of these estates, when the local women gave us a party. Another evening was spent visiting resettlers' families with handicapped children, when we were entertained in homes.

The day of the 10th anniversary of Chernobyl was especially memorable. On the previous evening, news had reached us of a fire at the reactor, causing fears of further pollution, but the day went ahead as planned. Morning worship at the conference centre was an emotional time for many local women. We then went by coach to the new Orthodox church in the resettlers' area and began tree-planting ceremonies in the Garden of Hope. All around was rough ground – the large-scale complex is still unfinished. Conference delegates were joined by the priest, nuns and members of the congregation. Sometimes it was hard to manoeuvre because of the press! Fifty fruit trees were planted and also flower seeds.

Late that afternoon we set out to join the public memorial march to mark the 10th anniversary – but it proved to be more than that. The Chernobyl anniversary had been hijacked by the People's Front, who were demonstrating against the country's move towards alliance with Russia. The Chernobyl group, now numbering several hundred, had been advised to take a different route and not to carry banners. The main route was blocked by soldiers with riot shields. The Chernobyl marchers assembled for a rally by a sports complex, but the main action and noise was not far away.

Moving to the edge of the crowd, I saw a man with bad head wounds and two young men with torn clothes and minor injuries, who had been roughed up by Russian soldiers. We later learned that two battalions had been sent from Moscow to control the march, which had exceeded 50,000 people. Two hundred had been arrested and dozens badly hurt. People seemed pleased to hear an English voice, and a young man said to me, "You are so fortunate to have democracy in your country." He was a lawyer.

Back at the centre that evening, the conference continued with a plenary session. We did not realise that two soldiers were behind the screens, monitoring our proceedings. Some of the local women feared they would be arrested, but all arrived home safely.

On the final afternoon we visited the Khatyn Memorial complex, scene of the notorious war-time massacre when 149 villagers were burnt alive by the Nazis. Khatyn is a memorial to all the Nazi atrocities committed in White Russia. Altogether the country lost one in four of the population during the Second World War.

I thought that I had done my homework before going to Belarus – the scientific picture was generally familiar. What came as a surprise was the political aspect. I had not realised that, with the increasing Russification of Belarus, Chernobyl problems are being played down. For five years young doctors and nurses were removed from work in the contaminated areas; now they are obliged to go there. Resettlers are being asked to return.

There is also the more subtle problem of control of information by the state and the fear that people who speak out could lose their jobs. Although her university work may have been at risk, one mother joined the memorial march out of concern for her children's future. An independent survey revealed that of voluntary agencies in Belarus the Children of Chernobyl Foundation (the largest) is considered the most effective. Yet it has been dubbed fascist by its political enemies, and there are anxieties about its future.

The closing sessions of the conference were devoted to practical problems such as alternative forms of energy, the disposal of nuclear waste and the human costs of energy policies. The barriers to progress were seen as only political in character, not technological, and international cooperation was seen as essential, so that there would be "no more Chernobyls, anywhere, ever".

We parted sadly from our new friends and sisters, but we were full of admiration for their faith and dedication. I hope one day to return and see how the trees are progressing in the Garden of Hope.

Shortly after the events described, the headquarters of the charity were raided by the KGB and records were seized. The charity was closed down and some of its leaders had to flee the country. Work to assist victims of the Chernobyl disaster is continued today by many groups and individuals both in the British Isles and on the Continent.

The Gospel for the Day
(A Preacher's Tale)

I had been invited to conduct a Women's Anniversary service on Passion Sunday. It seemed a difficult assignment, but the Gospel for the Day, the anointing of Jesus by Mary of Bethany (John 12: 1–8), seemed a promising approach. I worked on the passage, made a comparative study of similar accounts in the other Gospels, and became intensely interested. A sermon was planned. A few days before the service I made the long journey to the Network Day at Amesbury. The theme was to be 'The Mary in us' – and I was hoping for further illumination!

But in the event I was chasing the wrong Mary, as the Network Day focused on Mary, the mother of Our Lord. The worship materials, presentations and banners were inspiring, but of no direct use for the Sunday theme. As the weekend approached I completed the sermon and wove various strands from the Network Day into the worship. The day came and the service went better than I deserved. The congregation at Milford seemed amused at my admission of having gone in search of a different Mary. I drove home through the April mist and a few hours later we were on the first stage of our holiday, leaving behind Mary of Bethany – or so I thought.

The next day we were on a plane to Malta. About mid-journey I became aware of a conversation in the row behind us. An elderly man with a loud voice and a Yorkshire accent was enthusing about the Gospel for the Day, which he had just read in church. All around heard him telling the story of the anointing of Jesus by Mary of Bethany.

"It were spikenard – pure nard, not lard," he explained.

I thought, 'How wonderful! He's gossiping the faith, like Bunyan's women.'

It later emerged that he came from Bedford! Ted was one of our party.

"Then that Lazarus," he continued, "he told her off – said the money should have gone to help the poor. But really he wanted the money for himself."

Now here was a problem: should I join in? Wasn't it Judas Iscariot who told her off?

I struggled to my feet, stood by the drinks trolley, and joined in the chat: "Yes, we were thinking about Mary of Bethany yesterday as well." But I didn't say we were both in pulpits!

Then our friend started commending the lectionary to all around, saying how good it was that all churches should have the same theme. I thought how remarkable it was that so many years later, high above the Alps, even among strangers and travellers, Mary's action was still provoking comment. And I recalled the words of Our Lord: "Wherever the gospel is preached throughout the world, what she has done will also be told, in memory of her" (Mark 14:8). Truly a woman to be remembered!

The Darfur Years

All the recent news and images of Darfur have evoked memories of a chapter in our family history, as that was where our younger daughter worked for two years after leaving university. Her first sortie to Africa had been to Southern Sudan during a summer vacation back in the mid-eighties, when she had been helped by a generous gift from the Basingstoke Rotary Club. With a group of Oxford undergraduates, she had travelled to Yei to provide badly needed equipment for a school for Ugandan refugees. They had to fly over areas where there was sporadic fighting, but the full fury of the long civil war in the south was yet to come.

For her second sortie, our daughter returned under a scheme sponsored by the Sudanese Government. A party of new graduates flew to Khartoum – many, like Abraham, not knowing where they were going – and were allocated to the regions. Liz went to El Fasher in the Darfur region, employed to teach English. There were sixty to seventy students in a class. Jane Austen's *Pride and Prejudice* was on the curriculum. The president of the country at that time – a descendant of the Mahdi of Queen Victoria's time – was a liberal with an Oxford education.

There is a saying that once you have seen the Nile you have to return, and so it was with our daughter. By this time she had learned some Arabic and was becoming interested in development work. She arrived back in Khartoum, uncertain how she was going to get to Darfur, but the Red Cross labels on her luggage secured her a lift on a tiny two-seater plane.

For the next year, she helped set up and train women's health committees across the vast region of Northern Darfur – including in villages we have been seeing on our TV screens. At that time, the post took at least three weeks to arrive. There were no satellite communications, and no mobile phones, as there are today. Her Christmas presents and cake had to be organised well in advance.

The experiences of those years helped shape her career, and that was where she met her future husband. A good number of friends from the Darfur years gathered at their wedding celebration at our Southbourne church, including the Russian prince who was working as an aid consultant.

Liz left the Sudan amid rather dramatic circumstances. The Nile was badly in flood, with people stranded on the roofs of their houses. The Red Cross arranged for her to be interviewed for TV news on arrival at Heathrow. She had left a country whose old order was passing away. The more liberal, pro-Western government was being replaced.

We should perhaps not have been surprised when, exactly twenty years later, Liz returned to Juba, together with her Southern Sudanese husband, Korby, to take up a new appointment with the Department for International Development. She had been appointed to head the Joint Donor Team of like-minded countries which, working together with the World Bank, supports schemes for reconstruction and development to implement the 2005 Comprehensive Peace Agreement, which ended the war in the south. A joint initiative managed by the Dutch, the team also includes members from Denmark, the Netherlands, Norway, Sweden and the UK. With the international focus still very much on Darfur, their quiet dedicated work towards the Millennium Development Goals continues virtually unnoticed by the UK media and politicians.

From time to time I return to a favourite book, Thomas Pakenham's *The Scramble for Africa*. Comprehensive and compelling, it offers an insight into the background events which helped to shape African countries, including the Sudan, whose boundaries embrace a vast land and differing peoples.

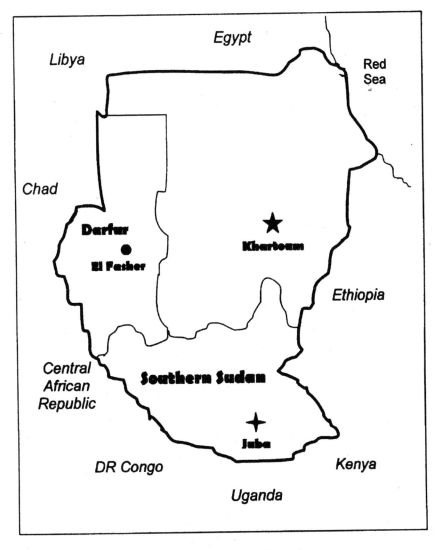

Map of the Sudan

Golden Memories
(July 13th 2006)

Ministers approaching their special wedding anniversaries this summer have been recalling the protracted difficulties with officialdom surrounding the lifting of the ban on marriage for probationers. Today's Methodists will be aware of more diverse and flexible arrangements for ministerial training, but prior to the mid-fifties the general ruling was that ministers should not marry until after ordination.

Many men had been in the services and could see no reason for the restriction. At the time it had seemed particularly hard for the wives-to-be, who had to wait perhaps six years before starting a family. But this was all about chaps in colleges who must not be distracted from their studies by marriage and – er – etc.

Increasingly there were murmurings in the colleges, agonised private discussions and petitions to Westminster – all apparently to no avail.

Then quite suddenly, it seemed, the restrictions were partially relaxed: Methodist probationers would be allowed to marry after leaving college. Hence the 'gold rush' of 1956 when, judging by the columns of the *Methodist Recorder*, a significant number of probationers were married just before starting their circuit ministry. The long wait was over.

Rightly or wrongly, it was rumoured that the heatwave during the 1955 Manchester Conference had helped to mollify entrenched attitudes!

Three years earlier than expected, Peter and I were married

at my home church, Shirley Methodist Church, Croydon, by the Reverend Fred Pratt Green and the Reverend Donald Lee, who had travelled from Oxford for the occasion. With characteristic kindness, F. P. G. would accept no payment and tore up the cheque. On our preliminary visit he mentioned that he had just been to see the play *Waiting for Godot*. Having another wedding, he was unable to attend our reception, but later he and his wife dropped into my humble home to have tea with assorted aunts and uncles.

It rained on our wedding day and on every day of our honeymoon in Scotland – although I do recall some serene sunny hours on Iona. All too soon the holiday was over and duty called.

We travelled separately to our first appointment. As the train drew into Hungerford Station I saw a solitary figure standing on the platform, holding a small brown-paper parcel.

He was T. D. Barnes, the much respected circuit steward. He welcomed me and handed over the fruit cake his wife Ada had made for us. Thereafter we were to know much hospitality and generosity from our new friends around the Hungerford circuit.

There was no manse for us, so we were housed in a small ground-floor flat. Peter had charge of five village chapels and was under the able guidance of the super, the Reverend Donald Collier (son of S. F. Collier of the Manchester Mission), who still had the stamp of the army about him. We had left behind the cities and the ivory towers and realised that we had a lot to learn.

Distant Adventures of Distant Cousins

1. MISS HARRIET

Recent family-history research has revealed some remarkable distant relations, such as Miss Harriet Kölkenbeck, who was born in Belfast in 1867. At the age of twenty-one she went out to China to work with the China Inland Mission, serving for forty years in the far-west province of Szechwan. She and her colleague faced many dangers and hardships, eventually having to leave China because of the troubled state of the country. Harriet died in London in 1940 at the home of her brother Frederick Kingston, businessman and evangelist.

The following letter recounts a narrow escape at the time of the Boxer uprisings. It was written by the Reverend C. H. Parsons, and published in Volume XXII, No. 21 of *The Missionary, at Home and Abroad* in September 1895.

Pao-ning Fu
East Si Chuan
June 9, 1895

The riot took place on Tuesday, June 6th at 10 p.m., a fine moonlight night. It was the great "Wun Tsu Huei," or gathering in honor of the god of Pestilence, when people from miles around crowd into the city. A secret society could hardly have selected a better time. Furthermore there had been a great drought; the rice is withered up in the waterless fields, and a good deal could not be planted out at all. Then again, news recently came of the great riot in Che-tu, the capital of this province, when all the stations (four missions, including the R.C's) were destroyed, – the missionaries being concealed in the Hsien Yamen. All these things, together with the news (now pretty widely known) of China's thorough humiliation in the war, tended to make it a very favorable time for attacking foreigners. All day guests had been coming and going, appearing friendly enough. In the evening I took the Enquirer's Class, and spoke about persecution, etc. Just after the gates were locked for the night, stones began to be thrown over the wall, and Mr. Williams sent off a man privately to the Yamen to tell the magistrate. Meanwhile the blows grew heavier, and the stones more frequent; then it settled down into a regular attack with loud cries of "ta-keo" (beat the dogs). Just as the outer gate gave way we got over to the Girls' Day School, the ladies having preceded us. Our party consisted of Rev. E. O. and Mrs. Williams, their three little ones (the youngest only two months), Miss Kölkenbeck, Mr. W. C. Taylor, and myself. Then we heard the yells of the mob who, breaking open the inner gate, demolished the railings before the private house, and then attacked the house itself.

We commended ourselves, and especially the little ones, to our Father in Heaven, but the mob seemed to get nearer and nearer, and using tremendous force, (probably battering rams) broke open the large gates of the chapel courtyard, and were soon at the work of destruction. Just at that moment the Mandarins arrived, – the military Mandarin, the Fu and the Hsien. The soldiers drove back the mob and took five prisoners, but it was some time before order was restored, and then the Fu and Hsien Mandarins came down to us to the school. They expressed sorrow for what had been done, saying it was the fault of the thoughtless country people who had come in for the feast, and then they invited us to make a tour of inspection with them to see the amount of damage. I stayed to keep guard over the ladies, for even then some daring fellows were continuing the attack on the chapel. The courtyard around the house was strewn with glass, and huge stones weighing 10 to 15 lbs were found in the rooms. Very few things, however, were taken; I lost both my Chinese beds, some cash and a foreign lamp. The servants lost the most. One dear old evangelist told me afterwards how the Lord preserved him. While in bed he saw two young fellows enter his room and seize what they could, whereupon he lifted his heart to God, and "the Lord hid him," for they went out, not perceiving that he was there. After the inspection the Mandarins sat down and discussed matters, the runners standing about the door, and men with lanterns being stationed in the courtyards. The Fu at once sent off messages to Kuang-yuen, to Pa-cheo, and to Tsang-his Hsien, in which district our Sanatorium, "Sin-tien'tse" is situated, to warn the Mandarins there. Next he asked us to go to the Yamen for a few days, as the next day would be "the great day of the feast," when the country people just pour in from daylight. So having spent the rest of the night in getting our things together, the officials got us 5 chairs and we left in the early morning.

Passing by the debris of our broken railings and gates, we were hurried through the already crowded streets, the Mandarin's chair leading the way, and runners being about us in case of trouble. We three men were taken to the Fu Yamen, while the ladies and children went to the Ting-li Yamen adjoining, whither the sisters from another house which had not been injured had preceded them. We are in splendid quarters, occupying what is called the "Flowery Parlour," a fine room, 44 feet by 18, with a carpet in the center, two full length mirrors, and two of the finest Rochester lamps I have ever seen. Some beautifully mounted scrolls hang on the walls, and a foreign clock stands on a side table. In front is a little courtyard with plots of green shrubs, and moveable awnings above to keep off the sun. The Fu came to see us on our arrival and bade us welcome. Mr. Taylor was allowed to leave for Sin-tien-tse, as he was anxious about the ladies who are there alone except for Chinese teachers and servants. The 5 ladies and 2 children are not so well off, being, I regret to say, in inferior quarters – two small rooms with a mud floor. We wish we could change with them. The little boy sleeps with me. The Mandarins at once set about repairing the house, employing 13 carpenters; it is now finished and they are doing the chapel.

2. THE BOYS GET DOWN TO WORK

The following extract is from *A Sketch* by E. S. Millidge (1956) (Emma Sophie Kölkenbeck), telling the remarkable adventures of her family.

At an early age, about 13 or 14, our father Hermann and his brother Joseph left their home on their "Wanderschaft" [travelling] to seek work in Belgium. It was the custom in those days for young men to do so in order to find work or gain experience in their trade or calling. These two young boys went to Liege where they found situations as junior clerks and having hired a room, chalked across the floor in half – one side marked 'Hermann' and the other 'Joseph'. Here they lived and studied diligently, teaching themselves French and other languages, bookkeeping etc. There were no evening classes in those days, (c. 1839–43). It was wonderful how these two young boys kept themselves and got on so that my father could later on correspond with great proficiency in 8 languages, including Russian. Uncle Joseph also prospered in business and married the daughter of a Lutheran clergyman. He and his family settled in London later.

The two boys who drew a line on the floor were from a Catholic background, but later adopted the Lutheran faith of their wives. During their time in Belfast, descendants of Hermann converted to Brethren beliefs. Joseph, my great-grandfather, married Clara, a pastor's daughter, and their family remained in the more liberal Lutheran tradition. Joseph died in 1915 and was buried at Camberwell, South London.

3. SOME CHRISTIANS IN RUSSIA

Shortly after returning from a Baltic cruise, the highlight of which was a visit to St Petersburg, it was quite extraordinary to learn that some distant relatives had lived there in the late nineteenth century. I had photographed the Church of the Saviour of the Spilled Blood, site of the assassination of Tsar

Alexander II, never knowing that this event would be mentioned in the homely family history, *A Sketch*, which we later received from distant 'new' cousins. Emma Sophie takes up the story:

... Our parents then both left the British American Chapel in St. Petersburg, which they had hitherto attended (probably the most evangelical 'place of worship' in that City at the time) causing no little stir among the other members. As our mother especially was a very bright Christian, she was greatly missed in the Chapel, especially by Mr. and Mrs. Nobbs who were among our parents' dearest friends. They were dear devoted souls who loved the Lord and served Him up to their light, opening their house to lonely English, French and German governesses and other strangers in that City who were employed in the many noble families resident there at the time. Such were free to come every Sunday afternoon to be entertained with great kindness and profitable conversation. Hymns were sung, one of Mr. Spurgeon's sermons read aloud, coffee and cake being served. These dear saints, the Nobbs, now long since with Christ, will not lose their reward for the valuable service rendered. They were quite elderly and Mrs. Nobbs had been like a mother to our mother who had come with young children as a stranger to a strange land. It must be remembered that just at that period there was some measure of religious liberty in Russia, the good Czar Alexander II being then on the throne. He was related to the British Royal family, favoured the Russian Bible Society, set free the Serfs, and was greatly beloved by the people in general, but was alas cruelly assassinated in 1881 by the Nihilists who were gaining power. On that very day, 13th March, the Czar had added his signature to a document of the first importance for the liberties of Russia. "With Alexander the Emancipator fell the hopes of Russia. Cruelly did the nation pay for that misguided crime" (see 'Under three Czars'). There was a great spiritual awakening in Russia of which little is generally known and many were the believers in that vast land helped and increased in number through the work of the devoted Stundists, of whom I cannot write now. That day will reveal it all. My father in his old age wrote an interesting little paper about these devoted servants of Christ.

Our mother was happy in St Petersburg, the servants and peasant class being on the whole, simple, honest, respectful and pious up to the little light they had. She learned enough of the difficult Russian language to read the Bible with the servants and talk to them and the trades people of Christ. Our father became an accomplished Russian scholar, this being necessary in his business. Three more children were born to our parents in St. Petersburg . . .

In November 1873 the family removed to London, our father having to go on before, reluctantly leaving our mother with the seven children, including myself a baby of 11 months to a trying journey in rough weather with a drunken captain, a disagreeable stewardess and on a vessel which proved to be unseaworthy – her last voyage – and no help except from God. Her devoted Russian maid Tatiana, who had been with her for six years, failed her at the last, being unable to tear herself away from her own aged mother; but God brought them safely through to London to our father who had found a house at 13 St. Paul's Road.

4. Lethal Weapons on a London Bus
As a girl I overheard some furtive Chinese whispers about a shadowy figure in the family, a mysterious uncle who was a seasoned traveller: who was he? There was talk of his having a collection of rare butterflies, and of his having been to the Arctic, but I was never put in the picture. The clouds of mystery descended again, and all questions were verboten.

It's been quite remarkable to learn more about my father's Uncle Charles in recent months, from our newly-discovered cousin. We've learned that shortly before the First World War Uncle Charles took part in the Tour du Monde, a race to traverse the world using scheduled services. The *Daily Telegraph* reported 'the latest record around the world by Mr. Charles

Kölkenbeck in 32 days, 17 hours' – a great achievement at the time. His family at that time were part of the Lutheran community in South London.

In 1948 his brother Ernst, my unknown grandfather, wrote that Charles had sometimes been mistaken for, and addressed as if he were, Winston Churchill. He was indeed a *great* uncle in various ways.

Many years after his uncle's exploits my father was turning out his attic and came across some hideous weapons which his Uncle Charles had brought back from the Gilbert and Ellice Islands. They were clubs about two feet long, made of a mahogany-type wood, entwined with leather thongs with sharks' teeth protruding. My father decided that these gruesome objects from the South Pacific were far too dangerous to keep in the attic in Croydon, so he took them to the Horniman Museum in Forest Hill.

Poor Uncle Charles! After internment in the First World War he was almost certainly deported, along with his elderly mother. We have letters saying how hard life was; how he was minded to return to England; and that Clara, my great-grandmother, had died in Berlin of a bee sting. We now know that Charles did return, and followed his family tradition of importing and exporting. His trade was in 'hats and hoods of every description'.

The jigsaw of our fragmented family history may never be complete, but it's been wonderful how painstaking professional research has transformed family mysteries into family histories. We have been enabled to discover new close relatives who were astonished to learn of our existence; but there is still a legendary figure we have been unable to trace.

Another 'new' cousin had longed for years to find some more Kölkenbeck relatives. This brave lady tells how she had to leave for the West at short notice, cycling through the Brandenburg Gate with no luggage, only the clothes she was wearing. A doctor in biology, Eva went on to work at a Canadian university. We met at a family lunch in London on Father's Day this year, and shared news and photos. It really was a case of genes reunited.

5. REMEMBRANCE

Writing on Remembrance Sunday, it's appropriate to reflect on the anomalies and follies of war, which affected my family along with many others. My father, Joseph Kölkenbeck, joined the army in 1917 and served in the 8th London Rifles (which he called the Post Office Rifles). He was captured by the Germans after just three weeks on the Somme and held as a prisoner of war at Merseburg, having to work on a farm and down a mine.

The prisoners were not ill treated, but faced near-starvation, having to eat grass and mangel-wurzels. The food shortage was dire, owing to the Allied naval blockade. The prisoners were given buckets of tea, and used to wash their mugs in the remaining tea!

There were many soldiers serving in the British Army who had German names; there was even a German Regiment. Many people had emigrated from Germany in the nineteenth century, either for economic or political reasons, or, in the case of my father's forebears, so that the sons could avoid military service in the brutal Prussian Army.

My father was a gentle, mild-mannered man, interested in music and art, history and world affairs. During most of his working life he was a minion in the Ministry of Works, and in retirement a keen supporter of music in Croydon. He had a special interest in Brahms, and was consulted for programme notes at the Fairfield Halls.

It was ironical that he should have been held at Merseburg, not far from Leipzig, where (as we now know) his father had been born. At the same time his father, a non-combatant, was held in Germany with English people, due to his English connections, being listed as 'stateless'. And Uncle Charles was almost certainly detained in London, due to his German connections, along with thousands of others.

My father changed his name by deed poll in 1920, taking the name of Franklin, as he was an admirer of Sir John Franklin, the Arctic explorer. He only unburdened himself and told us his hidden history late in life. It seems that he had been kept in a sort of mental prison, but he retained letters, papers and objects linking him to his past. I still have his cherished Bechstein piano, made in Berlin.

6. A Bridge-Builder in Bridgend

I'm also reflecting on the story of Frederick, brother to Miss Harriet, the missionary, a go-between evangelist among many other things. Frederick, a talented linguist, pursued a range of trades in London, including book publishing, printing and translation. Books published by Frederick can still be bought on the Internet. In *A Sketch* his sister Emma Sophie tells of his remarkable ministry after the end of the Second World War:

> Between 1946 and 1948 our brother had a wonderful opening among high-ranking officers of the German army who for some years after the War was over were confined in a prison camp at Bridgend, S. Wales. Through a Brother (i.e. a member of the Brethren Sect) who catered for the camp he obtained easy access and was able to hold a good many Gospel meetings with these officers, who but for the marvellous arranging of God, would have been quite inaccessible to the ordinary visitor. He spoke the simple Gospel to them in their own tongue, telling them in the first meeting of his own conversion when a little boy in Germany. They gave him a very warm reception begging him to come again as soon as possible and he believes that God crowned this effort with His distinct blessing. It meant a long journey from Barnet to Bridgend Camp and back at the age of 76 or so, but he felt it was worth the effort!

It was not the first time that Frederick had acted as an evangelist in a post-conflict situation. As a young man he had gone to South Africa on business in the years following the Boer War and he used to preach and hand out tracts. *A Sketch* was written from a Brethren perspective.

Did my father ever know about Frederick, born with the same name, who lived only ten miles away in the London suburbs?

Probably not. But it has been our privilege to learn about him, using the Internet, from a new distant relative in the Yukon Territory! The adventurous Kölkenbeck tribe spread far and wide, especially in North America, but many changed their name to Kingston at the time of the First World War due to the climate of opinion, and now the name has disappeared in England.

The study of family history, begun earlier this year, has had some of us spellbound, making us feel very close to our forebears. But it has been disturbing as well. In these days of prosperity, openness and freedom of thought, few of us can appreciate the hardships and hazards, crises and moral dilemmas of former times. We can only hope that life has moved on.

Part V

WORDS FOR WORSHIP

Amazing Grace
(A Reflection on John Newton)

Amazing grace (how sweet the sound)
That saved a wretch like me!
I once was lost, but now am found.
Was blind, but now I see.

Newton's powerful and passionate hymn is undoubtedly the best representation of his life and faith. It's set to an early American melody from the plantations – perhaps originally from Scotland. At the height of its popularity, some decades ago, it was often played by bagpipes, and sounded quite good – though some may disagree!

But what of the words? 'Amazing grace' – powerful, passionate and poetic! 'Amazing' seems to be the in word at the moment, especially among young people. When declared Sportswoman of the Year, the Princess Royal used the word four times in her short speech of acceptance. But 'amazed' is very much a biblical word. When they heard about the camel going through the eye of a needle the disciples were exceedingly *amazed* at Our Lord's teaching. When as a boy he was found in the Temple among the teachers, everyone was *amazed* at his understanding and his answers. When Jesus healed the boy with the evil spirit, all were *amazed* at the greatness of God.

But what was so astonishing in the story of John Newton? He lies buried at Olney in Buckinghamshire, and here is the inscription on his tombstone: 'John Newton, clerk, once an infidel and libertine, a servant of slaves in Africa, was, by the rich mercy of Our Lord and Saviour Jesus Christ, preserved, restored, pardoned, and appointed to preach the faith he had long laboured to destroy.' These words were written by Newton himself, for posterity. He often told the story of his conversion, and never failed to marvel at the great turnaround in his life.

'Once an infidel and libertine'. Now, John Newton's mother was a godly woman, but sadly she died before he was seven. He went away to school for a few years, then joined his father's ship when he was eleven to begin life as a seaman – but later, alas! he lapsed into a life of rebellion and debauchery. He served on several ships and at one stage escaped, but was recaptured and flogged with the cat-o'-nine-tails, and degraded from his position as midshipman on the quarterdeck.

'A servant of slaves in Africa'. Newton worked on several ships and also worked on the islands and coast of West Africa, collecting slaves and selling them to traders (we have heard the story of how Equiano and his sister were kidnapped). At one stage he was the servant of a slave dealer and was made to plant lime trees. Eventually Newton became a captain of his own slave ship, transporting slaves to the West Indies and America – a cruel and vicious way of life. One of the abiding memories of our visit to Ghana was to be taken to Elmina Castle on Cape Coast – one of a number of fortresses along the coast – where slaves were held before being crammed into the ships. I remember the chilling dark dungeons with low ceilings, and the narrow gap in the thick wall, called 'the point of no return', through which the captives had to pass sideways on their way to the ships. Our guide explained that pregnant women were not allowed on the ships. And for a while Newton was part of this process, this unspeakably cruel trade. It was part of a triangle of trade, involving sugar, armaments and those who were regarded as less than fully human – labour for the plantations.

John Newton 'was, by the rich mercy of Our Lord and

Saviour Jesus Christ, preserved'. I never cease to marvel at the risks people took in sailing the seas many years ago – including the Wesley brothers – but a particularly violent storm, when it seemed that all would be lost, proved to be a turning point in Newton's life; it was during a storm at sea that John Wesley felt his own lack of faith. Newton began reading the devotional book by Thomas à Kempis, *The Imitation of Christ*. He was preserved from the violent storm and challenged by the message of the book. And these experiences at sea were used by the Holy Spirit to sow the seeds of Newton's eventual conversion. Later he wrote his hymn, based on the prayer of King David:

> Through many dangers, toils and snares
> I have already come.
> God's grace has brought me safe thus far
> And he will lead me home.

This was his hymn for New Year's Day, 1773 entitled 'Faith's Review and Expectations'.

Newton was 'preserved, restored, pardoned' and began inwardly to change. For some years he continued as a slave-ship captain, trying to improve conditions and even holding services for the hardened crew. But he must have felt very uncomfortable with his guilty conscience. We can perhaps see an analogy with St Paul, who some while before his conversion had gathering doubts about whether he should persecute Christians.

Eventually our hymn writer felt convinced of the inhumanity of the work he was doing and turned his life around. After leaving the slave ships due to a mystery illness, he became Tide Surveyor in Liverpool, and married Mary Catlett, his childhood sweetheart. During his nine years in Liverpool he felt the call of God increasingly to preach the gospel and to study for the ministry.

He was 'appointed to preach the faith he had long laboured to destroy'. Newton was greatly helped and influenced by John and Charles Wesley, and by George Whitefield. For six years he sought ordination and eventually it was the Bishop of Lincoln who ordained him and appointed him curate at Olney. And so he became a pastor and a very popular preacher. Large crowds gathered to hear the 'old converted sea captain'. And he was an innovator, too, preaching in other buildings outside the church. 'Fresh expressions' didn't start in the twentieth century!

There was a need for new hymns, too, as the old psalms seemed too staid, and Newton wrote a new hymn for each Sunday evening service. And so the volume of Olney hymns began to be written: 282 by Newton himself, and 67 by the poet William Cowper, his friend and neighbour. After the annual pancake race at Olney there's a service in the Parish Church, during which 'Amazing Grace' is sung – and other Olney hymns.

After fifteen fruitful years our hymn writer said, "My race at Olney is nearly finished." He had been offered a living as Rector of St Mary Woolnoth, in the City of London, and it was here that he spent the last twenty-eight years of his ministry. Many of his converts went on to do great things for the Church. The former slave trader was continuing to campaign against the slave trade, working with William Wilberforce and other political leaders for its abolition. The campaign went on for many years, and the leader, Wilberforce, was especially vilified. William Cowper wrote a sonnet in his support. The Act was finally passed in 1807: slavery was to be abolished in British territories. And it was in this same year that our hymn writer, John Newton, passed away, aged eighty-two. He never ceased to marvel at God's mercy and grace, which had so dramatically changed his life.

Very appropriately, 'Amazing Grace' is the theme of the 2007 Methodist Prayer Handbook. For some while I was puzzled by the picture on the front. It's a painting by Rembrandt depicting the parable of the prodigal son, who has returned to his father's house. In his ragged clothes he's kneeling in repentance and being comforted by his ageing father. And the well-dressed elder brother is looking on. Surely this is a wonderful illustration of God's grace in action – just as it was in the life of John Newton. The lost son was preserved, restored and pardoned.

John Newton's epitaph reminds us that he was saved 'by the rich mercy of Our Lord and Saviour Jesus Christ', by the self-giving of Jesus on the Cross. It was by God's love in action. God's grace is active and ongoing, available to us day by day. As Protestants we believe that the grace of God must be accepted as a free gift – it is not something which we can earn.

Someone has asked, Is God's grace only for bad sinners with dramatic and colourful lives? And is it something magic which comes through the formal services of the Church? Rather it is a relationship which comes to any of us, which we have to be open to receive. A minister in New York has written: 'If what we call our spiritual life is becalmed, and our little ship of faith lies limp in the harbour of our daily round, we have to be there, with sails hoisted, when the wind of the Spirit blows' – alert for the signs of grace which come to us in unexpected places.

It would be possible to regard the Olney hymns of Newton as inward-looking and not concerned for the world – but this would be misguided. Through his change of heart there was a change of lifestyle, and along with others he worked for the abolition of the slave trade. Using all his powers and influence, he made a difference.

The slave trade today exists in different forms and includes forced labour, child labour and the trafficking of women and girls; not all this is in the developing world, but much is on our own doorstep. And so there is an ongoing need for all Christians to educate themselves and others about these contemporary abuses of human rights, and to work towards a better world.

At Spring Harvest the question was asked, "Does grace produce change?" In John Newton's case, it did! ". . . true grace will revolutionise our lives. It will not just leave us as comfortable Christians, socially irrelevant to the world around us. We will be changed by an encounter with grace."

Scripture references
1 Chronicles 17:16–17; Ephesians 2:8–9

Bibliography
By the Banks of the Ouse – Olney Parish Church
101 Hymn Stories, Kenneth W. Osbeck, Kregel Publications
An Anthology of African and Caribbean Writing in English, edited
   by John J. Figueroa, Heinemann and Open University –
   'Equiano on his Way to Slavery'
The *Expository Times*, July 1982, p.306, Reverend Dr David Read
Methodist Recorder, April 22nd 2004, report on Spring Harvest
Other Olney papers
Paul – Envoy Extraordinary, M. Muggeridge and A. Vidler,
   Collins, p.46
Companion to Hymns and Psalms

A Closer Walk with William Cowper
(A Reflection with Readings)

William Cowper lived in the eighteenth century, at approximately the same time as John and Charles Wesley. He wrote reams and reams of poetry, including many translations from Greek and Latin poets. He also wrote lots of letters, and sixty-seven of the Olney Hymns. Some of Cowper's words are still quoted: 'God moves in a mysterious way' is perhaps his most famous phrase from a hymn. 'I am monarch of all I survey', often quoted, is the opening line of his poem to Alexander Selkirk, the sailor abandoned on an island for five years, who was the inspiration for the Robinson Crusoe story. And there's another phrase, which circulated in our household when the children were young:

> What peaceful hours I once enjoy'd!
> How sweet their memory still!

I first encountered William Cowper many years ago when he was on the syllabus for an English-literature exam, so I saw him first as a poet, having at that time less interest in hymns. He pronounced his name 'Cooper'; and his family coat of arms depicted three hoops, the emblem of the cooper. He was known as Sir Cowper to the more humble inhabitants of Olney. But who was he exactly, and what did he do?

READER: Cowper was neither a philosopher nor a theologian, but he was certainly a poet – which is more than can be said of a good many hymn-writers. With typical

97

modesty he dismissed his merits as a poet: 'I have no more right to the name of a poet than a maker of mousetraps has to that of an engineer; but . . . I have often wished myself a good one . . . It has served to rid me of some melancholy moments.'

In a letter written in 1792 Cowper gave his correspondent a brief autobiography, worth quoting as revealing the character of the man: 'From the age of 20 to 33 I was occupied, or ought to have been, in the study of the law. From 33 to 60 I have spent my time in the country, where I was sometimes a carpenter, at others a birdcage maker, or a gardener, or a drawer of landscapes. At 50 I commenced an author. It is a whim that has served me longest and best.' *

Cowper was born in a country rectory in Hertfordshire. He was described as 'shy, tender, timorous and affectionate'. But tragedy struck when he was six: he lost his mother. Straight away he was sent to a boarding school, where he was bullied unmercifully. He was later withdrawn from the school at Berkhampstead and at the age of ten was sent to the Westminster School, where life was better. He had a physical deformity – a 'thorn in the flesh' – and with this and his nervous disposition he seemed scarred for life. In his long poem, 'The Task', he described himself as 'a stricken deer that left the herd'.

It used to be said that Cowper suffered from bouts of madness; but perhaps now we would see these as mental or nervous breakdowns caused by situations of stress. He seems to have had an innate ability to recover, and his various periods of melancholy led on to times of healing and light. At the age of twenty-one his sadness was dispersed by a visit to Southampton.

READER: His religion was sincere, if misguided. He had more than one conversion experience. In his twenties, while sitting near an 'arm of the sea which runs between Southampton and the New Forest', the gloom lifted from his heart. It was a calm morning, with the sun shining on the sea, and, to quote his own words: 'On a sudden, as if another sun had been kindled in the heavens on purpose to dispel sorrow and vexation of spirit, I felt the weight of all my misery taken off. My heart became light and joyous in a moment.' As he was later to write:

> Sometimes a light surprises
> The Christian while he sings;
> It is the Lord who rises } Malachi 4:2
> With healing in his wings:
> When comforts are declining,
> He grants the soul again
> A season of clear shining,
> To cheer it after rain.

I suspect that these gleams of unexpected light, these seasons of clear shining, were more frequent and of longer duration than many of Cowper's biographers allow. *

In his early thirties he needed to apply for paid work, and a suitable vacancy was well within his reach, as clerk to the House of Lords. But the thought of interviews and exams caused a serious breakdown and he tried three times to take his own life. His misguided religious beliefs had convinced him that he was marked out for eternal damnation.

READER: Cowper was transferred from London to Dr. Cotton's Home for Madmen at St. Albans. Here he lay strapped to his bed, gibbering his delusions of eternal damnation. He felt the flames and heard the shrieks of hell. But in spite of his fragile nervous system there was an innate vitality in him which enabled him not only to recover, but even to eke out his almost three score years and ten. And as his madness took the form of damnation so his recovery expressed itself in the joyous assurance of salvation. He was a brand plucked from the burning.

This phrase, so meaningful to Methodists, prompts the question, did Cowper ever meet the Wesleys? If he didn't, more's the pity, as their preaching and belief in salvation for all would have reassured the insecure poet. The Wesleys were a generation older: at the time of their conversions Cowper was a little boy of seven, being bullied at school. There seems to be no record in John Wesley's journal of his having met Cowper. But we learn from Wesley's private diary that, when he was too ill to preach, on several occasions he read the poetry of Cowper whilst on his travels.

A further breakdown occurred when Cowper was engaged to be married. The marriage never took place, and for the rest of his life he lived with Christian friends. He enjoyed a close friendship with his neighbour the Reverend John Newton, the former slave-trader, who was Rector of Olney. The two men were of very different dispositions and some have even questioned whether the friendship was good for Cowper; but it was Newton who encouraged him to write hymns, and this proved a kind of therapy. The two men had another bond: Newton too had lost his mother when he was six, and had been sent away to school.

Cowper loved the countryside – "God made the country, man made the town" – it gave him peace and consolation. He loved his circle of close friends and became a great letter-writer. His letters give a fascinating insight into his life and times – for example, the surprising number of arson attacks. His writings range from learned translations of Greek and Latin poetry to tales of trivial domestic incidents, recounted in grand manner, often with gentle humour. We hear about his pet hares and kittens, and there's a delightful long poem called 'The Retired Cat'; she was shut in a chest of drawers all night in her master's bedroom. Then there's a poem complaining about the price of fish, and another about a box of oysters lost in the post. Perhaps his most famous piece is 'John Gilpin', a hilarious ballad of more than sixty verses, which has given much pleasure to many people.

William Cowper, country gentleman, was not narrow in his

outlook and interests. He was a philanthropist and a satirist, and he was interested in the issues of his day. He aligned himself with the anti-slavery campaign, and he wrote a sonnet in support of Wilberforce. He felt guilty about using sugar – and thought of the cost at which it had been produced.

READER: From 'The Negro's Complaint':

> Men from England bought and sold me,
>   Paid my price in paltry gold;
> But, though slave they have enrolled me,
>   Minds are never to be sold. . . .
>
>   . . . Think, ye masters iron-hearted,
>   Lolling at your jovial boards,
> Think how many backs have smarted
> For the sweets your cane affords.

Our closer walk with the poet has come to an end. We have seen him as a fragile and complex personality, one for whom faith comes and goes, and one who struggles to find meanings in life's events. His hymns are drawn from biblical verses – perhaps mainly from the Old Testament – seeing God as great but mysterious. Many people can relate to him today as his faith ebbs and flows, from certainty to searching.

READER:
> God moves in a mysterious way
>   His wonders to perform;
> He plants His footsteps in the sea
>   And rides upon the storm.

* * * * *

> O for a closer walk with God,
>   A calm and heavenly frame,
> A light to shine upon the road
>   That leads me to the Lamb!

And so we have walked with William Cowper, hymn-writer, man of letters and 'the most English of poets'. We owe him an apology that the bicentenary of his death was not widely observed in the year 2000 – perhaps because we were all so busy celebrating the Millennium.

* these extracts from 'God Moves in a Mysterious Way: William Cowper' by Peter G. Jarvis have been used with the author's permission.

Bibliography

The Poetical Works of William Cowper, edited by H. S. Milford, OUP, 1905.

Cowper: Poetry and Prose, edited by H. S. Milford, OUP, 1921.

Companion to the School Hymn-Book of the Methodist Church, W. S. Kelynack, Epworth Press, 1950.

The Journal of John Wesley, Vol. VI, 19th and 20th March 1783, Epworth Press.

The Expository Times, May 1969, 'William Cowper' by H. Wilson Curry.

The Expository Times, June 2003, 'God Moves in a Mysterious Way: William Cowper' by Peter G. Jarvis.

After the Marriage at Cana

The story may be read from the Dramatised Bible (John 2: 1–11).
In the reflections which follow, the speakers are introduced by a
narrator.

MARY:

The angel told me this would be a very special child. As Jesus
grew up he did all the things that boys do. He enjoyed life, but
he had a serious side – always asking questions, he was. Then,
when he was old enough, he began to help his dad in the
workshop. He lived at home for many years: then he began to
travel as a preacher. But those questions! Yes, he always had a
serious side – and hidden powers which kept surprising us.

One day we all got invited to a wedding. It was a huge affair,
with lots of family and friends. Jesus came late, along with His
new friends – His special gang. But something awful happened:
there were so many people at the feast that the wine ran out – so
embarrassing for the family. I thought, 'I really must do
something' – my cousins were in such a flap – so I turned to
Jesus. I thought He'd be able to come up with something. He
seemed rather short with me – it was very hurtful. Then He said
a strange thing: "My hour has not yet come." I didn't understand,
but I let it pass.

So I said to the servants, "Do whatever He tells you." I just
knew that He could and would do something to help. So He
gave instructions to the servants – and you know the rest of the
story. It seemed that the water had become wine. It was a wedding
feast no one will ever forget, and the family were not put to
shame because the supplies had run out.

A DISCIPLE:

It was a very exciting time, going to the wedding feast with Jesus and the rest of our group. By the time we arrived, the celebrations had already been going on for several days: and there were so many people there that the wine ran out. We hoped it wasn't our fault, for swelling the numbers.

So Jesus's mother turned to Him for help; she really embarrassed him, like mothers do. He seemed rather short with her – "Why turn to Me?" – but of course she often turned to Him, being the eldest son, after His father had died. And then He said something very strange: "My hour has not yet come." What hour? What did He mean? Anyway, not long afterwards there seemed to be plenty of wine for all, and we realised that this was a spectacular sign, and we believed in Him. Later we saw many other signs.

THE WINE-MASTER:

It just seemed to be an ordinary village wedding. We thought we'd got everything under control, but as the week went on far more people turned up than we'd been expecting. It was very hot, so everyone drank a lot, and really enjoyed themselves – though the wine was watered down, of course. As for what really happened, I only heard about it afterwards, and I felt really humiliated. They told me that the original wine had run out, but suddenly there was lots of new wine in the big water pots – as if the water meant for cleansing had become wine. It seemed that Mary and Jesus had something to do with it, so the servants told me later.

Anyway, I went to compliment the bridegroom on the good wine he'd been keeping till the end, not knowing the full story. He seemed happy enough that everything had gone well – but I was pretty annoyed and embarrassed when I heard about the crisis, I can tell you.

A HOUSE GROUP MEMBER:

I don't really know what to make of this story. It's the most challenging part of the Gospel for me. Of course, I realise that they had to drink wine in those days, but they must have been overdoing it if the supplies ran out. Fancy Jesus turning 120 gallons of water into 120 gallons of strong wine! I'm strictly TT so I've got a big problem with that, but I have to believe it as it's in the Bible.

ANOTHER HOUSE GROUP MEMBER:

Well, I don't have a problem with the wine – that's not a big issue for me. But there are some other funny things about this story. Why did Jesus say, "My hour has not yet come" and then go on to perform a miracle? And then, what really did happen? Did a miracle really take place, or was everyone only pretending, just to spare the host from shame, and as a result the gossip about a miracle got spread around? As I said, the wine-drinking isn't a problem for me; it's simply that I find the story hard to believe – and why is it only in John's Gospel?

ST JOHN:

My friends, I'm afraid you are both missing the mark. You're both getting hung up over factual details, and taking it all too literally – whether you believe or disbelieve the story, you're missing the real point. In my stories there are always hidden meanings and different levels of truth. You need to search for clues – they are there in plenty.

For example, there were six stone jars. Now, seven is the perfect number, so six suggests that before Jesus came life was not yet full and complete. Life under the Jewish law could be compared to water, but Jesus brought the glorious new wine of the Gospel, and He brought it in abundance.

Then again there are several clues which point to the coming death and Resurrection of Jesus. This story is like a cameo – it's a miniature picture of the whole Gospel. The wedding banquet reflects the joy of the Kingdom of God; the wine shows abundant joy. Jesus brings a joy which nothing before could achieve. This story is all about how Jesus manifested His glory.

JESUS:

I AM THE GLORIOUS NEW WINE.

PRAYERS OF CONCERN

Intercession

God of all lands,
we pray for places in the news –
places of disaster, devastation and death –
and for places forgotten.

God of all peoples,
we pray for people in the news –
people whose lives have been disrupted,
people in doubt and despair,
people who feel forgotten.

Reconciling God,
we pray for all who feel guilt
at the hurt they have caused to others,
or because of the way they have
mismanaged the lives and trust of others.

Forgiving God,
we pray for all who have feared
or neglected to challenge corruption and evil;
and for ourselves,
as we have compromised the values of your kingdom.
Give to all your people integrity, healing and hope,
and enable us to share these gifts with your damaged world.
In Christ's name. Amen.

Bind Us Together

God, your church is where ordinary people gather
with all their varying needs –
women and men,
young and old,
simple and capable,
sinners and saints,
poor and rich.
Hear us, heal us and bind us together, O Lord.

The church is where your gospel is proclaimed
and your truths discussed, week by week
in word and sacraments,
in mid-week fellowships,
in dialogue and debate.
We pray for all who preach and lead us in worship,
and for ourselves in our daily witness to Christ.
Hear us, heal us and bind us together, O Lord.

Many come seeking refreshment and renewal:
some are overworked, others are unemployed;
some are lonely, bereaved or sad;
some are successful, others are disappointed;
some have illness, stresses, or anxieties about others.
Hear us, heal us and bind us together, O Lord.

Through your church we find newness of life,
light, joy and laughter,
and all the richness and variety of your gifts to us.
Help us to use your gifts more creatively.
Hear us, heal us and bind us together, O Lord.

Reproduced from *Living Prayers for Today*, compiled by Maureen Edwards,
1996, with the permission of the International Bible Reading Association.

A Prayer for Special Places
(Written on Hengistbury Head, Dorset)

Creator God, we thank you for the special places in these islands:
for the sites where ancient peoples once dwelled,
and for the skills of those who explore and reconstruct their lives.

We thank you for sites of special scientific interest,
and for the insight of those who preserve endangered species
of animals and plants.

Give wisdom to those who seek to reconcile
the conflicting claims of conservation and tourism.
Show us all how to value and enjoy your Creation,
to educate and inspire the young
and to preserve our places of special heritage
for future generations.

An Intercession

God of all lands and peoples,
we pray for those whose work takes them to distant places,
to help with relief and development
among needy and damaged communities.
Grant them safe journeys
and sustain them in their ongoing work
at the interface with other cultures.
We pray for their parents
and for all who carry burdens of anxiety
about distant loved ones.
May they find support and succour in their communities of faith.

An Offertory Prayer for Juniors
(Written for Christchurch, Mudeford Lane)

    Silver coins, five-pound notes,
    Hidden cash in envelopes;
    Bags of money, bags of care,
    Offered now, your love to share.

SHORT SKETCHES FOR SUNDRY SERVICES

The Face at the Window
(A Drama for Juniors, Written for Christchurch & Lymington Circuit Celebration, June 15th 2003)

Exactly three hundred years ago a very special boy was born. His name was John Wesley, but his parents called him Jacky.

The Wesley family lived in the big Rectory at Epworth in Lincolnshire. It was a wild, flat, damp countryside.

Samuel Wesley, John's father, was the Rector and he was in charge of the church.

John was one of a large family, with lots of brothers and sisters.

Sometimes Samuel Wesley used to quarrel with the people in the village, and was very strict with them.

One night a terrible thing happened at the Rectory: some rough men from the village set fire to the Rectory to punish the Rector, and all the family were in danger.

There was a dreadful panic as all the family tried to escape from the fire.

ALL BROWNIES & CONGREGATION: Fire! Fire! Help! Fire!

Some of the family got out through the windows, and some through the back door. The maid brought out the youngest, who was called Charles.

Susanna and Samuel Wesley began to count their children. They realised to their horror that little Jacky was still there in the burning house.

They could see his face at the window. He was shouting and

crying out for help.

ALL: Help! Help! Save Jacky! Help!

All the friends and neighbours wanted to help, but there was no time to find a ladder, as the fire was so bad.

Then one man climbed onto the shoulders of another, so that he could reach the window, and little Jacky was lifted to safety.

Soon afterwards the roof collapsed, but little Jacky was safe; and his parents and all their friends gave thanks to God.

Jacky's mother, Susanna, said some words which have been remembered ever since: "Is this not a brand plucked out of the burning?"

Although he was only five years old when all this happened, John Wesley never forgot his narrow escape from the fire, and his mother's special words.

ALL READERS: As he grew older, John Wesley came to realise that God had some very special work for him to do.

Props: A 'window frame' in the pulpit. Orange scarves.

Home from Home

(Written for Methodist Homes Sunday,
Barton-on-Sea, November 2005)

Scene   A cafe somewhere on holiday
Characters Kathy (a care assistant)
             Betty
             Jo(e) (Betty's brother or sister)

KATHY: Hello there! Do you mind if I join you?
BETTY: Of course not. Do join us. I'll move my shopping.
       Hasn't the week gone quickly?
KATHY: It really has – but have you enjoyed it?
JO: Well, most of the time. But we've had a big worry.
BETTY: We had to leave mother in a special home – she's
       not so well these days – she gets confused and upset
       – but it's only for one week.
JO: But as I've said, it may have to be for longer.
BETTY: Definitely not. I feel dreadfully guilty about
       abandoning her and coming on holiday.
KATHY: But you mustn't feel guilty. Most of these special
       homes are really first-rate. They really care for each
       person as an individual.
JO: That's what I've tried to say – and we may have to
       face it – it may have to be permanent.
KATHY: They look after people with all sorts of problems:
       some are just elderly and frail; some are blind or
       deaf, or disabled; some have dementia – their minds
       are failing – they're in special units.

JO: Well, that's just what I fear is happening to Mother.

BETTY: Rubbish! You have senior moments yourself sometimes.

KATHY: Well, I'm sure your mother's in the best place and you will all make the right decision. There are wonderful new facilities to cater for people's different needs – and state-of-the-art accommodation. You mustn't feel guilty.

BETTY: You seem to know a lot about it.

KATHY: Yes – actually I work in a care home. It's a Methodist home in Yorkshire – but there are over sixty around the country.

BETTY: Methodist? Aren't they the people who sing hymns?

KATHY: Yes, among other things! – lovely friendly people to work for and with. The place where I work has won an award. Oh, and hymns are a good thing, by the way. Some of the residents may be elderly and forgetful, but hearing an old hymn can jog their memories. They join in, and seem to know all the words.

JO: Well, I think that would suit Mother fine. She used to love all the old hymns.

BETTY: Well, yes – it sounds quite a good idea, I have to agree.

A HANDFUL OF HYMNS AND SONGS

Tune: 'My Love's an Arbutus', Irish traditional.

Vision of Peace 1

I dream of a time when the world is at peace,
When neighbour loves neighbour and warfare shall cease,
When beauty shall flourish and justice increase:
I dream of a time when the world is at peace.

Oh, make me, Lord Jesus, a channel of your peace:
Unblock the unworthy, your Spirit release;
May your goodness flow to others, that all tensions may ease:
Oh, make me, Lord Jesus, a channel of your peace.

Tune: 'Morning Hymn' or 'Tallis' Canon' L.M.

Vision of Peace 2

(Written for Troubadours for Peace, Blackpool, 2007)

This special day, with deep concern
We meet to pray, to hear, to learn;
Our mutual love and hope to share,
Our vision for a life more fair.

Aware of hunger, grief and greed
We see the world in all its need –
Yet dare to pray these wrongs may cease,
For only justice leads to peace.

Transforming God, we wait the time –
The end of hate, oppression, crime
When all enjoy more peaceful days,
Respecting one another's ways;

When all shall live in unity
Yet cherish rich diversity;
And when, to fullest stature grown,
All humankind your way will own.

Renewed in vision, joining hands,
Children of God across all lands,
We pray there may in us begin
The lasting peace which starts within.

Tune: 'Bethany' or 'Hyfrydol', 8.7.8.7.D.

The Charles Wesley Hymn Writing Challenge, 2007

Give us words to sing your praises,
Give us music to inspire;
Harmonies and tunes and phrases,
Words for pulpit, pew and choir,
Words of faith and revelation,
Words to sing and words to say,
Words of prayer and proclamation –
Word Incarnate, here today.

Give us hearts that feel contrition
For the scope of human sin;
Anguish at the earth's condition,
Sorrow for the wrong within.
Through the greed which knows no limit,
Through suspicion, fear and strife,
Speak to us, rebuking Spirit,
Guide us to a fairer life.

Give us hands to reach to others
As we travel on life's ways,
Pilgrim sisters, pilgrim brothers,
Sharing bright and darker days;
Hands of peace and affirmation,
Hands for service glad and free,
Raised in praise and consecration –
God Eternal, Trinity.

Tune: 'The Lord's Day'.

Hymn for a Special Anniversary
(Written for the Highcliffe Centenary Year, 2008)

This is the place,
This is the place where we come to sing,
Where we come to sing.
We will rejoice,
We will rejoice as we come to sing,
As we come to sing.
This is the place where we come to sing;
Praises and thanks and blessings bring.
This is the place where we share God's grace.

This is the place,
This is the place where we come to pray,
Where we come to pray.
We will rejoice,
We will rejoice as we come to pray,
As we come to pray.
This is the place where we come to pray,
Seeking the Lord's strength for each new day.
This is the place where we come to pray.

This is the year,
This is the year when we celebrate,
When we celebrate.
Gathering here,
Gathering here let us celebrate,
Let us celebrate.
This is the year when we celebrate;
Sing to the world that our God is great.
This is the year when we celebrate.

In Celebration of the Wesleys

We celebrate two brothers
Who joined, in student days,
In fellowship with others
For study, prayer and praise;
By discipline of living,
With holiness their aim,
From such a small beginning
A mighty movement came.

We celebrate their mother,
A saint beyond compare,
Who led them to discover
The faith they had to share;
Who toiled, and taught, and preached, and prayed –
For her no life of ease –
And in due time her blessing gave
On ventures overseas.

We celebrate the poet
With writings manifold,
Who by the Holy Spirit
Brought treasures new and old;
To waiting congregations
The words of life were given;
With glad anticipation
They sang their way to heaven.

We celebrate the preacher
Outside the church's door;
Exhorter, pastor, teacher,
Befriender of the poor;
All tirelessly he travelled,
Escaped from storm and flood;
And faced with hostile hearers,
Courageously he stood.

We join in celebration
Of two whose voice was heard,
And reached the common people
By music and by word;
And as we now remember
Our cherished heritage,
We seek for fresh expressions
To serve our present age.

IRRESISTIBLE AFTERTHOUGHTS

Old Jeffrey
(Strictly not part of the Hymn Writing Challenge)

We celebrate Old Jeffrey
   (now was he man or beast?)
Appearing in the Rectory
   to greatest and to least;
In multiple disguises,
   a friendly spirit, he
With strange sepulchral noises
   did haunt the family.

The Rich Man and the Poor Man
(Based on Luke 16:19–31, written for Highcliffe Harvest,
October 7th 2007)

A story told in Galilee
    two thousand years ago
Has meaning for us all today
    and shows what we should do.

The story goes a rich man lived
    in luxury complete,
Designer clothes in rows and rows
    and lots and lots to eat.

Not far away a poor man lay
    just longing to be fed;
The rich man never noticed him
    and never gave him bread.

The poor man to the rich man said,
    "Of food I've not a scrap."
The rich man to the poor man said,
    "That's your bad luck, old chap."

The poor man to the rich man said,
    "You really are a hog."
The rich man to the poor man said,
    "I need to feed my dog."

The two men parted company
    and went away to dwell;
The poor man went to paradise,
    the rich man went to hell.

The poor man sat with Abraham
   and found content at last;
The rich man watched and envied him
   across the chasm vast.

The rich man said to Abraham,
   "It's getting rather hot,
Please let me have a nice cold drink" –
   but Abraham said not.

The rich man thought, 'I'd better warn
   my family and friends,'
But sadly this was not allowed –
   and there the story ends.

This story shows that having wealth
   does not bring happiness:
It's better far to share good things
   with people in distress.

The meaning of this ancient tale
   is plain for all to see:
That those with wealth should show concern
   for those in poverty.

And so for us at harvest time,
   across the human map,
With neighbours near and neighbours far
   we'll work to mend the gap.

Guidelines for Poets

The Hymn Writing Challenge said
'vigorous',
The Southlands song had to be 'rigorous'.
For hymn or for song
Which was right and which wrong?
The general effect was to jigger us.

The answer to the crossword clue on page 60 was RIPPLE
(*Daily Telegraph* Crossword No. 24,218, November 21st 2003).

126